We're Not in

YOUTH GROUP

Anymore

We're Not in
YOUTH GROUP
Anymore

C. S. Morris

WHALER
BOOKS

Buena Vista, VA

1 3 5 7 9 10 8 6 4 2

Library of Congress Control Number: 2025906593

We're Not in Youth Group Anymore
C. S. Morris

p. cm.
1. Religion: Christian Education—Adult
2. Religion: Christian Living—Personal Growth
3. Religion: Christian Living—Spiritual Growth

I. Morris, C. S., 1995– II. Title.
ISBN 13: 978-1-966392-02-6 (softcover : alk. paper)
ISBN 13: 978-1-966392-03-3 (ebook)

Design and Layout by Karen Bowen

Whaler Books
An imprint of
Mariner Media, Inc.
131 West 21st Street
Buena Vista, VA 24416
Tel: 540-264-0021
www.marinermedia.com

Printed in the United States of America

This book is printed on acid-free paper meeting the requirements of the
American Standard for Permanence of Paper for Printed Library Materials.

Contents

Chapter 1
Knowing Ourselves

"Remove the dross from the silver, and a silversmith can produce a vessel..."

–Proverbs 25:4

L et's be real, **we aren't kids anymore**.

Up until now, most of our lives have been structured for us. Whether that structure comes from our parents, school, extracurricular activities, etc., it doesn't really matter. We, for better or for worse, have had other adults dictate a lot of our lives, our schedules, and our environments. The same can probably be said of our spiritual lives as well.

Believe it or not, though, becoming a legal adult doesn't magically make us mature individuals. Maturity is not a byproduct of age; it is the result of the attitudes and behaviors we develop based on the wisdom we have gained from our experiences and the interactions we've had with those around us. If we want to become mature individuals, we must first have a good understanding of ourselves, others, and our perceived place in the world.

The Pew Research Center conducted a study in 2014 where they called more than 35,000 people to ask different age groups how likely they were to attend religious services. People between the ages of 18 and 29 were the least likely group of people to attend church. This group also had the smallest percentage who said they attended church regularly compared to groups that went seldomly or sporadically throughout the year. This trend has only continued upward post-COVID.[1]

There are a lot of reasons why people leave the church throughout their lives, but there is a significant drop-off at the age where we gain independence from the structures we are used to. Coincidence? Maybe not.

We are responsible for our own growth, but how can we grow if we've never been given the tools to do it? I believe the modern church is learning how to do a better job of teaching people in this transitional stage of life how to better steward their own faith into a foundation that will last a lifetime…but that kind of change takes time.

I appreciate all of the work that many churches put into engagement with youth, but, in my experience, most of the time that hasn't translated into a development of identity, life skills, or a transformed worldview. Then, we get pushed out into the real world where we suddenly discover that faith and a relationship with Jesus aren't based on ice cream parties, singing songs, dancing, or other forms of entertainment with a little bit of Jesus or a quotable Bible verse sprinkled in. We are expected to figure out a place to live, get a job, decide whether or not to pursue higher levels of education, make big financial decisions for the first time, navigate new relationships with people who are different from us, and sometimes while moving away from family and friends within a very short time span.

At this stage we are expected to have a faith strong enough and developed enough to help make those decisions and overcome these new obstacles. However, I think at some point the question needs to be asked, has that kind of faith actually been developed? How do I develop it if it wasn't? How would I continue to grow in it, even if it was developed, now that it is my responsibility to do it on my own? Do I know how to study scripture on my own? Do I know how to "take it to God"? Am I capable of dealing with the discomfort that comes with growth?

I can remember advice from others to "continue reading the Bible and pray," and while it is well-intended, that advice sometimes wasn't helpful. It felt passive when it actually came time to face some of my first challenges as an adult. I wanted real advice and help, but how do I get it? Who do I talk to? I was not in a youth group anymore, and in my case, I had moved away to a new place to attend college and didn't find a new "home church" until six years after high school. Even then, it took time to build up relationships and trust with those I met at church to feel comfortable asking for guidance in my life.

I didn't want a relationship with God that was really just a relationship with other people who knew God. I wanted my own <u>real</u> relationship and a faith that I could trust and rely on. I wish I'd had the knowledge and answers I do now about God, about myself, and about the things I wanted then—but I didn't. I also understand that a lot of those kinds of answers come with time, but that is why it is important to start some of those conversations now and to spend time getting to know and challenge ourselves in our faith and beliefs, which is what I hope to accomplish in both halves of this study. The first part of this study is going to focus on how we interact with ourselves. Starting with our perception of ourselves.

Most people I know and have observed live in a cycle of perception that looks a little bit like this:

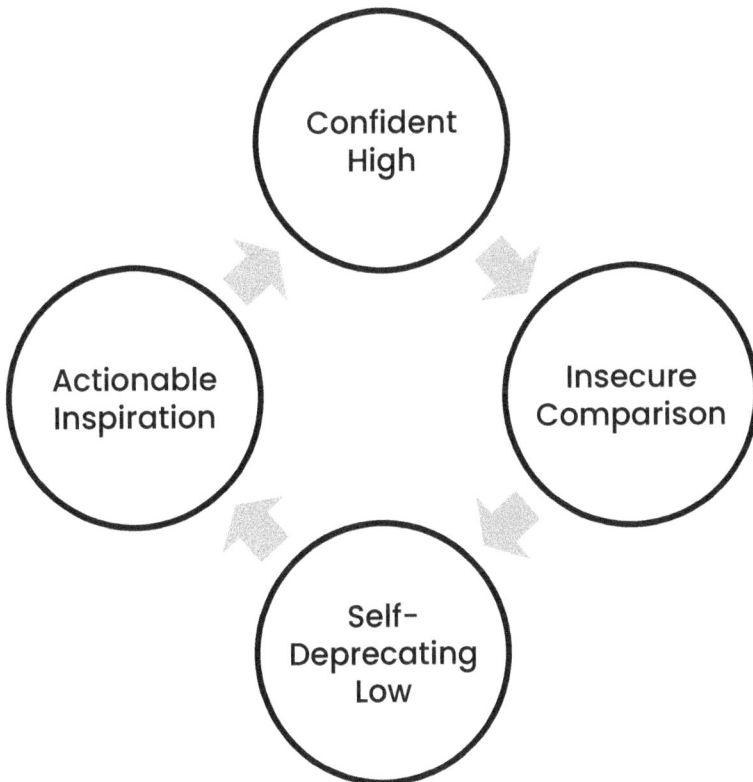

Confident High

Insecure Comparison

Self-Deprecating Low

Actionable Inspiration

The first stage is the version of ourselves that is riding the **Confident High**. This is the powerful feeling, best version of us that can slay the dragon, land the dream job, have the right comeback, make the funniest joke, and look effortlessly fine while we do it. It is predictable that moments like this usually correlate to times in our lives when things are going great. We feel in sync with our environment; maybe we have recently gotten good news or accomplished a goal we've been working towards for a long time, or we've made a new life-changing decision that we believe will put us on a path for a better future, and we feel invincible. The world is our oyster and full of endless, positive possibilities. We have purpose, drive, excitement, and a plan for success.

Everyone, to some degree, wants to be on this high, and they strive toward it in their social or spiritual lives. Some people seem capable of living their entire lives in a high confident zone. Our favorite celebrities, influential leaders, or maybe someone in our everyday lives just always seems to be floating on a cloud that none of us can reach. However, the truth is that we are all human, and while the highs are good while they last, there is an end to them.

It is an unrealistic and unreasonable expectation that anyone can maintain that standard for themselves. The idea that the confident high version of us should be the standard is a lie that plenty of people are willing to sell to us, and this leads to the next phase in the self-image cycle, the **Insecure Comparison**.

Over time, the confident high self-image can become a source of torment:

"I need to look better."
"I need to be recognized more."
"I need to be stronger."
"I need to be more put together."
"I need to be making improvements or reaching the next milestone."

Definitely the kind of thing that would keep us up at night or tempt us to push ourselves beyond our capabilities. The comparison game is *sneaky*. I think we see the comparison game often talked about as a way to recognize petty jealousies over things like looks or social status, but what about comparisons that sound like:

"Why haven't I reached my goals yet?"
"Why do I seem to have to try harder than everyone else to succeed?"
"Why can't I get it together?"
"Why do I struggle to find people to love and support me in the way I need?"
"Can't everyone see how hard I am trying?"
"Why won't God help me?"

We start to compare our efforts and expectations with our results and find them lacking. This can be frustrating, disheartening, and maybe even depressing. Suddenly, under the weight of comparisons and insecurities, the image we have of the high self eventually gives way to the **Self-Deprecating Low** version of ourselves.

The self-deprecating low version of ourselves is the rock bottom self-image. This is the us that feels the ugliest, the dumbest, the most ignored, and the least cared for. This is the version of us that sees all of our flaws in the worst possible light and then ruthlessly condemns us for them. We start doubting or questioning whether or not God really cares. We believe that there's something wrong with us. We obviously are not as special, as talented, or as blessed as our peers.

Maybe we've stopped taking care of ourselves and have allowed our lives to become a mess. Oh, and don't forget that everyone else can see it—that must be why they've stopped caring about us or investing in us. Maybe we even have people in our lives who encourage a line of thinking that says we just aren't disciplined enough or that we haven't tried hard enough to maintain the high. So, we begin to beat ourselves up to set goals or to "get better."

Eventually, we do begin to build our confidence back with small victories like being able to clean the dishes in the sink, taking care of ourselves by showering a little more frequently, eating healthier, or starting a new regimen or curriculum of some kind. This is the fourth phase in the self-image cycle, **Actionable Inspiration**. The smaller victories build upon themselves and give way to the bigger ones, like maybe losing those ten pounds, getting a raise at work, or achieving a major life milestone. We start to ride the high again. *"I knew I could do it if I just tried harder."*

There are always going to be times in life where, to achieve our goals, we have to pick ourselves up by the bootstraps and keep trucking, even when it's difficult or hard, to see the fruits of our labor. However, this is a place for discernment. Are you working hard and taking measured steps to achieve a goal that is based in faith, or are you trying to force yourself to meet an unrealistic standard or timeline? Have you accomplished these goals with the help of the Lord or through your own power alone?

The problem is that the actionable inspiration leads to the confident high, which reinforces the cycle and the idea that our actions and accomplishments are what form our identities and are the source of our self-image and not the consequence of it. An example of this difference in thinking might look like: "I did a kind act today; therefore, I am a kind person," versus, "I am a kind person; therefore, I took action today." The issue with the first line of thinking is that our actions or achievements determine our identities or values instead of the other way around. This doesn't hold up when we start to have thoughts like:

> *"Do people only like me and care about me now because I'm acting or looking the way they want me to?"*
> *"What happens if I fail?"*
> *"What happens when I can't bring something of value to the table?"*
> *"What if the work I put in to be this person was a lie or not enough?"*
> *"The real me is the low version of me. No one likes them, so I will work extra hard to not be like them anymore."*
> *"I can be the high version forever if I just try a little more,"*...until we can't, and the cycle starts back over again.

The truth is that the high version of us and the low version of us, while both possibly true representations of how we can be, are not a standard or an expectation to hold ourselves to, no matter how comfortable or tempting they may appear. There's a more realistic, everyday version of us where we will spend the majority of our lives floating between the highs and the lows and that needs to be based on an identity that is rooted in Christ, regardless of circumstances. I'm hoping that by challenging ourselves in healthy and controlled ways, we can start the process of reframing or reaffirming the self-image cycle from the one above to look more like the one shown here.

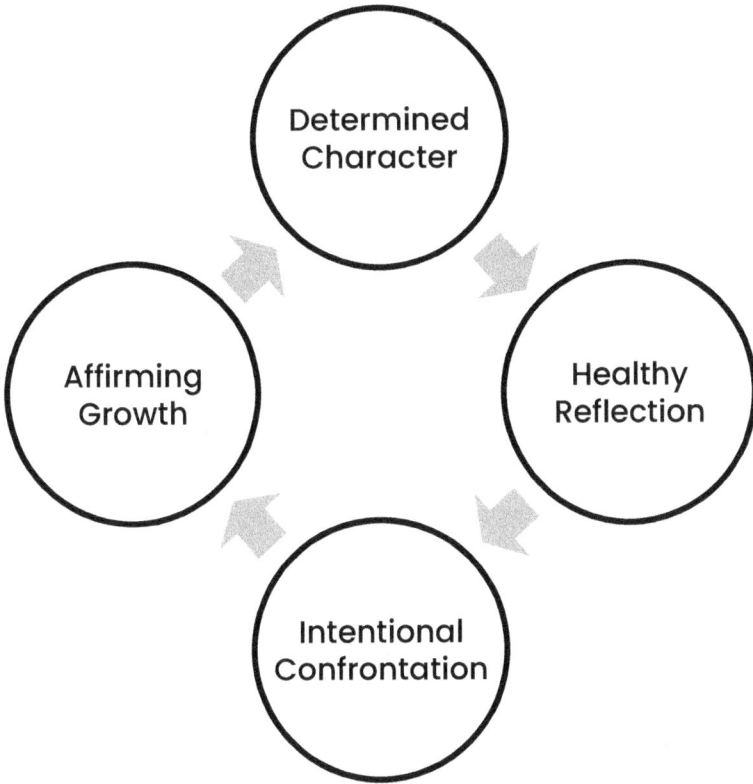

The goal of this self-image cycle is to prompt and promote positive growth by beginning to view ourselves as ever evolving and growing individuals who are rooted in Christ and willing to submit to His refinement process. Basically, it's the cycle of becoming comfortable with growth and change to help establish an unshakeable identity and achieve our goals.

It is important to begin growth from a place of stability and security. When we stop and take stock of God's values and the personal values we have for ourselves, we are able to build a blueprint for what we want the foundation of our identity to look like. First, we determine the type of person we are, the person we want to be, and if we are willing to face challenges to become that person. This is the step of deciding on the **Determined Character.**

The reason we determine the kind of character we want at the beginning is so that we can have a clear vision and purpose moving forward when we begin to face those challenges that would prevent us from becoming the kind of person we are determined to become. We need to know it is okay to go through hard things, to look at our weaknesses, and to examine past hurts so we can learn how to move forward from them. The Lord promises to be with us through all trials and challenges, and we will not be growing alone (Rom. 8:35–39, Isa. 43:2). When we have that confidence going into the process, we are already starting from a strong and sound foundation. It helps to operate with that locked-in mindset of safety and assurance to face the harder things in life.

The second step in the cycle is **Healthy Reflection**. Once we feel confident and secure that we know what we want our foundation to look like, we need to identify the areas that we need growth or maturity in to discover what prevents us from being the person we have determined we want to become. Once we can pinpoint our areas of struggle, we need to find a way to investigate why these areas hold us back. Is it a fear or insecurity that we have, an unresolved trauma, or do we have limitations that keep us from the growth we want to see?

Either way, the things we need to look at shouldn't be the results of our comparisons to anyone else but ourselves and the realistic characteristics we want to have as a person. For example, maybe I know I want to be someone who is kind and self-controlled, but I know I have repeatedly acted in a reactionary or impulsive way from a place of anger. I recognize a need to figure out why this is a problem. No one is a saint, and everyone gets angry, but if it is something that habitually holds me back from the things I want to do or the kind of person I want to be, then I should recognize it as something that needs to be confronted and addressed.

Once we have picked the area that we want to confront, we need to spend some time on the third step in **Intentional Confrontation** to determine what needs to change and why not doing so hinders us from being able to grow. The goal of this exercise is not to tear ourselves down or hack ourselves to pieces, but to take a controlled and purposeful look at our shortcomings to determine what it would take to overcome them in reasonable measures. We also need to determine if we are willing to put in the work to overcome them.

What would it look like to have a healthy relationship with the topic or challenge you chose? How do you bring this topic to God? What examples can you draw from the Bible that speak to this topic or limitation?

Is this something you can change on your own? If not, what resources do you need to seek out to help you overcome it? Is there anyone trustworthy that you can talk to about these issues? At this stage, try to be curious instead of overly critical, and spend time in introspective prayer. God is invested in our relationship, and He is good about helping us find answers to questions or prompting us in the right direction when we ask for His wisdom (Prov. 19:20, Matt. 7:7–12).

Once you have identified what you need to confront and reflected on why it is an issue for you, the final step is to take actions towards **Affirming Growth**. These are steps and actions that affirm the identity of the person we have chosen to be from the first step in the cycle. Seek out healthy paths of change, pray and ask God to help transform you or grow you in this area, set realistic goals, remove some of the obstacles that have been weighing you down, and take steps to get closer to the person you know you have committed yourself to be without having to rely on negative defenses or coping mechanisms.

This is also where you may get a trusted community involved. Ask for help, accountability, or prayer from the people you trust around you. Look into counseling options or mentorship programs. This looks different for everyone. It is not a race—you are building lasting foundations for *your* identity, not flipping a light switch. Change may happen slowly, but it will happen if you begin to take the right steps in the right direction.

Over the course of this study, we are going to look at eight different topics that I typically see people get stuck on or struggle with in their growth path and then review them together. Keep in mind that this study has been intentionally written to challenge you. It is not meant to be easy, and it is supposed to help you become comfortable with the idea of intentionally confronting yourself with areas you may be struggling with. If we aren't mature enough to push ourselves out of our comfort zone because it is what we are used to, then we will struggle to grow any further from where we are now.

Tradition alone wasn't a good enough reason for Jesus; it shouldn't be for us either. In His ministry, Jesus was quick to criticize leaders who clung to traditions over the spiritual health and well-being of those they were teaching (Matt. 23:1–36). The failure to take a risk to challenge the status quo of our current beliefs or habits because it is what we have been told or because it makes us comfortable is never a good enough excuse and should be at the very bottom of our list of reasons why we don't try.

The next four chapters of this study have more of a focus on our mindset when we make decisions or the perspective we have about ourselves. The following four chapters after that have a focus on how we relate to others in our environment and challenges that stop us from being able to live in community or put others into proper perspective.

In preparation for the upcoming chapters, contemplate the following questions and prompts:

1) Take some time in prayer and write out a list of characteristics you would use to describe your current self, both the positive and the negative. Then, write out a second list that describes the type of person you want to be and a list of characteristics you want to have at the foundation of your identity.

_____

_____

_____

_____

_____

_____

_____

_____

2) Spend some time before you start to pray and reflect on yourself and the two lists in front of you. What do you need to face or change in your life to be the person you described wanting to be above?

_____

_____

_____

_____

_____

3) Do you feel like God has highlighted anything to you recently as an area that needs growth? Write out a prayer asking God to show you what areas or topics He's interested in working on with you.

_____

_____

_____

_____

_____

_____

4) Write out a third list of struggles, habits, or shortcomings you feel currently hold you back or moments from your past that you want to be able to grow from.

_____

_____

_____

_____

_____

_____

5) What kind of work will be required for the things you listed above to be confronted properly and in a healthy way? Are you willing to put in that work to overcome the things on the list?

_____

_____

_____

_____

_____

_____

6) Are you open to feedback and accountability from trusted members of your community? What are some ways you can prepare yourself to share things honestly and receive feedback from your peers on topics that might be hard, sensitive, or speak to your current identity and beliefs?

_____

_____

_____

_____

_____

_____

Chapter 2
Risk

"Whatever you are not changing, you are choosing."
–Laurie Buchanan

One of the first crucial steps to becoming a mature Christian adult is learning how to take healthy risks. The Bible calls us to come boldly before the throne of God (Heb. 4:16), and from my personal study of scripture, time and time again, I see God choosing to partner with people who are willing to take risks and step out in faith and obedience to the things He has called them to do.

Noah spent his time and resources building an ark when there was no indication a catastrophic flood was coming outside of what God had told him (Heb. 11:7). Esther, in the face of an ethnic cleansing, went boldly to her husband, the king, and revealed herself as a Jew to save her people (Est. 7:3). Abraham, the father of nations, left his own father to travel and settle unknown lands (Gen. 12:1–4), and he was even willing to sacrifice the life of his promised son, Isaac, to God (Gen. 22:9–10). Daniel survived the lion's den after standing firm in his faith (Dan. 6:20–22). Peter asked to walk on water (Matt. 14:28). Rahab risked her life, and the lives of her family members, to help Joshua's spies (Josh. 2:12–15). David not only faced Goliath but was on the run and in exile for decades before he became king (1 Sam. 17:51, 2 Sam. 2:4).

Maybe we aren't royals or someone who faces lions and giants on a regular basis, but God honors the more subtle acts of courage too. Jesus calls out and honors the widow, who gave the last coins she had as an act of faith in front of the religious leaders who were giving more financially but risking very little personally (Mark 12:43–44). When her mother-in-law was widowed and childless, Ruth risked her future to stay with Naomi and care for her as a daughter instead (Ruth 1:16).

In big ways and in subtle ways, scripture shows God to be trustworthy, and even though it may feel uncomfortable, following His calling for our lives is one of the biggest acts of faith but also one of the biggest opportunities for partnership with the Lord that there is. Biblically, when someone took a big risk and it turned out for the better, it was partnered with faith and obedience to the Lord and His will. We need to trust God enough to have a healthy relationship with risk. The Lord is a big God who does big things, and He partners with us to do it when we are willing to follow Him.

What does a healthy relationship with risk look like? Maybe we can gain a better understanding of healthy risk by being able to identify what unhealthy relationships with risk look like. From my perspective, there are two main types of unhealthy relationships with risk. The first one is the kind of relationship where we are unwilling to take risks or we limit our willingness to take risks.

This perspective of being afraid to take chances is very much ingrained in our modern culture, particularly in the school age and the time just after we graduate from school. When we are constantly subjected to standardization in an overly competitive environment, risk becomes a luxury that we fear we can't afford. When adults ask us, "What do you want to do with your life or be when you grow up?" We hear the *actual* underlying question of, "What can you be successful in and make money at?"

In early and developmental childhood and adolescence, we are given narratives that tell us we need to start becoming athletes, scholars, and socially nuanced pillars of society **NOW**. We take the classes, engage in extracurricular activities to the level we can, and stuff our schedules as full as possible (whether we want to or not) on the threat that, without these things, we won't be able to compete with our peers when it comes to having opportunities for a good future or a happy life. That pressure to perform is only compounded if we know we are facing challenges that the majority don't face, such as financial distress, a lacking support system, a broken family life, mental illness, physical disabilities, etc.

This type of living and thinking leaves next to no room for actual self-exploration or dreaming. We think maybe when we are adults we will finally have the time to explore those things, but by and large, taking on new responsibilities, working a job, building new social relationships, etc., fills up our schedules in the same way and still doesn't leave much room for self-discovery. Stepping aside from the focus of making money and passing tests, we need to investigate ourselves. Do we know what makes us feel whole? Do we know what our talents, strengths, and weaknesses are? Do we have a calling for our lives? *Would we know it if we did?*

As an adult, I can now see that a lack of self-awareness and controlled risk-taking can sometimes lead to feeling like we can't make decisions on our own or properly gauge the actual stakes involved in taking chances. Some of the behaviors I see cultivated as a result of this mindset are most often tied to feelings of insecurity and doubt. This can look like constantly checking in with people who are viewed as authority figures to make sure we are doing things "correctly," refusing to spend time or resources on ourselves because we think we need to make and save as much money as possible, and limiting social interactions to people we already feel safe and secure with.

We are always deferring to others' opinions. We constantly need someone to tell us what to do or to agree with us before we will commit to an idea or decision in a way that shows dependency more than trust. Even in small ways and over fairly trivial things, the fear of being wrong or challenged keeps us from doing things like making doctor's appointments, meeting new people, pursuing hobbies, forming decisive opinions, or taking the time to properly rest.

I'm half convinced we do so much interacting online now because no one wants to face the fear of being perceived in the moment or take the risk of having to deal with the consequences of their words or actions face to face. Our best foot, or maybe the most protected one, must always be put forward. We design our image like armor to be what we think people want to see or hear to meet an unseen standard instead of being authentic and present in our environment. Not to mention, heaven forbid, we are *actual* human beings who make *actual* mistakes with *real* consequences; our fate is all but sealed. Jesus might as well go ahead and call us home right now because there's no way we could _ever_ recover from this error.

In all seriousness though, once this fear becomes a controlling factor in our lives, we circumvent the fear of risks by taking none of them, and this just leads us to an even more restrictive place because now others make the decisions for us. We will only go to places we know or that are recommended to us. We limit our vulnerability to what we know will be accepted or received well. All opinions or ideas become parroted from things we've heard someone else say they think. We surround ourselves in an echo chamber of people and opinions that are "like us" and feel threatened by anything new that would disrupt that environment. We're probably more likely to take the first decent-paying job or relationship and be resistant to branching out or change from fear of losing security.

It's okay to like some things the way they are and find comfort in traditions and known environments as long as we aren't becoming slaves to it. If we are, it can start to feel like we are stuck in the same miserable patterns, always doing the same things at the same places with the same people. We leave ourselves open to having our lives dictated by the whims of whatever authority figure we have given that control over to, even when we don't want to. Here's the deal: when it comes to us internally, nothing changes if nothing changes, but change will continue to happen around us externally, whether we are prepared for it or not.

This is the place where we usually get frustrated, because instead of feeling a purposeful control over our lives, it feels like life is happening *to* us instead of with us or for us. You can easily be pushed to a place of fear or anger when that "security" you have built for yourself is threatened or challenged by change. You may feel like choices have been taken away from you and that you are forced into your current position, but the reality is that you made a choice by not taking on the risk due to the perceived consequences.

Looking at the parable of the three servants in Matthew 25, Jesus talks about three servants who were given different portions of talents (money/resources) to steward while their master was away. The two servants who took the talents that were given to them and returned with them multiplied were honored and praised by their master. The servant who was too afraid to risk what he had been given buried the talent. When he returned with the same amount he started with, the servant was chastised and had his portion taken from him.

Keep this in mind when considering whether or not to take a chance on a calling the Lord has placed on your heart. Talents, like your resources or skills, can be buried underneath a job, an insecurity, a trauma, or a relationship just as easily as dirt. There are equal if not *greater* consequences to not acting and growing with the Lord, even when there is a risk involved.

Another biblical example of the consequences of refusing to take risks is in Numbers 13–14, when God tries to give the promised land to the Israelites. When they see that the land is already occupied by powerful people, they complain that the Lord has led them to their deaths and rebel against the Lord and their leaders instead of following through like God asked. For them, the risk was too great. As a result, they were never allowed to enter the promised land. Instead, they wandered the desert for forty years because they chose not to take the risk or to trust in God. In Matthew 19, a wealthy man is invited to follow Jesus if he is willing to give away his earthly riches to the poor. The man ends up walking away sad.

We do a disservice to both God and ourselves when we bury what is good about us or when we reject our ability to make decisions for ourselves based on the fear of worldly consequences. By not taking a risk for the healthy things we want or are called to, we are risking never being able to get to where we need to be. *It's a risk either way*, but at least if we do take the chance, we have the possibility of a different outcome than the one we are guaranteed if we don't. Do you have a desert you are wandering in because you won't enter into the good things God has for you or promises you?

This is what it means to walk by faith. If God has given you a direction or if there are actions you should be taking that align with scripture, but you are afraid to take the risk because of perceived consequences or because you don't know the outcome, you need to learn how to grow in faith and to trust in the Lord. If you find yourself struggling with that area of growth, then you need to start asking questions and exploring why.

The second type of unhealthy relationship with risk is the kind of risk we take because we are relying on ourselves to fulfill our lives more than we are relying on God. We can all think of moments or situations that we have been in where we felt hurt, uncomfortable, and maybe even angry or upset about the way our lives were going.

Maybe we perceive injustices in our lives that we feel like have gone unanswered or unaddressed. Maybe we have gotten tired of the same old things day in and day out that never seem to change. Maybe we are in an unhappy place in life and are desperate for an escape. We think to ourselves that we would do anything to change the circumstances we are living in if we were just given a chance. When you are faced with life-altering decisions or opportunities during times like this, you need to be careful. There is a *real* temptation to take big risks that could very much lead to consequences you aren't prepared for.

It may sound fun or exciting to hit the explosive reset button on our lives and dream about being able to walk away from our current issues to step into a life free of the burdens we are facing. The chance to take control of our lives like we never have before and become the person we always felt like we were meant to be is attractive to us. It may seem like we are finally getting our big, main-character moment where we are validated and justified in our feelings and all the hardship or monotony can be thrown into the wind. However, in reality, when these feelings are acted upon without being in alignment with the Lord, we can end up down an isolating and self-destructive path that is hard to walk down and hard to recover from.

There has definitely been a cultural movement in recent years towards transformation and maybe even some deconstruction. I am all for stripping away and changing the things that hold us back from our full potential or from the fullness of our relationship with God; we need change in order to have growth. However, we need to acknowledge that transformation takes time and oftentimes needs to happen internally in a healthy way before we will see the positive results externally. It is popular to cut out of our lives anything that we feel isn't serving us or making us happy in that moment, but sometimes life is about waiting out the storm instead of getting caught trying to run away from it.

No one can be in a permanent place of constant deconstruction without becoming unstable themselves. If you are in a genuinely harmful environment, please tell someone, seek help, or leave. Safety should always be a priority, but have enough self-awareness to know when you are being abused and mistreated versus uncomfortable facing life's hardships, unpleasantness, or challenges that come with change. Building a life on whatever makes me happy today usually comes at the expense of stability and emotional security tomorrow.

In my experience, when we hit the big reset button on our lives in the context of having a need to escape from life, it's because we are not fulfilled in some way on the inside, and we think that by starting our lives over on the outside, we can rebuild the "right way" where we end up feeling satisfied and whole. However, rebuilding on the outside changes nothing on the inside. I've noticed and identified in moments where I've gone for the big risks from an unhealthy mindset that fear, secrecy, and isolation come along with it.

I don't think it's a coincidence that the first thing Adam and Eve did after taking the risk on the fruit was to hide (Gen. 3:7–10). It feels defensive and even somewhat paranoid at times. We don't trust anyone to understand what we are going through. We don't allow the trustworthy people in our lives to support us, and in fact, we may go out of our way to keep secrets from them. We've already made our decisions and will not be taking anyone else's input right now, thank you very much, and that includes God. The only one who can be believed, trusted, or relied upon is ourselves. Whatever decisions we make, no matter how drastic or potentially hurtful, is just the truth we are walking in right now, and if the people around us have a problem with it, then they obviously never loved us or cared about us; they were just trying to control us or get something from us.

Hopefully we can see how very quickly we are not only destabilizing our lives but simultaneously cutting out our support system along with it. What we are doing is building a foundation for our lives on our ability to make ourselves happy or stable, and we will ultimately have the same problems we had before the blowup, even if they manifest differently. Whatever we feel like we are lacking physically, spiritually, or emotionally, whether that be validation, love, provision, security, worth, or anything else, our decision to cut all ties and walk away from healthy support systems won't suddenly give us those things, and we will continually try and fail to find ways to supply those things for ourselves in ways that are not in alignment with what God would have for us.

Change is constantly happening and constantly needs to happen, but it needs to happen in a way that is honoring to and in alignment with the Lord. We need to acknowledge that no support system can love and understand us perfectly all the time. Sometimes things don't go the way they were supposed to, and we get left without.

Accidents, mistakes, misunderstandings, shortcomings, and more happen every day, but that doesn't give us permission to take control to fix those things in ways that personally satisfy ourselves.

This is what it means to walk in obedience. If we are trying to follow the Lord, we can't take the reins and make things happen our way and in our own timing. Things like justice, restoration, love, purpose, clarity, understanding, and wisdom come from the Lord. We have to be willing to understand and act in a way that shows self-control, patience, love, peace, and humility during the times of life that are difficult and hard, not walk and not act impulsively within our own understanding.

When we are considering whether or not to make big changes or leave things the same, our mind focuses on all the things that can be gained or lost, but we need to consider what is actually at risk. God wants a personal relationship with us where we pursue our callings together, but God will complete His plans with or without us (Prov. 19:20–21). God designed us to be in partnership and in relationship, but the feeling has to be mutual. By His nature, God cannot force us to walk or work with Him when we have made it clear we would rather pursue our own interests and desires. There are examples in scripture where people have chosen themselves and their perception of security or power over their life callings from the Lord, and it has cost them dearly.

At the very end of Deuteronomy 32, God tells Moses that because he betrayed the Lord, he will not be allowed to enter the promised land, and instead Joshua is tasked with leading the Israelites after Moses dies. In 1 Samuel 2–3, God calls on Samuel to replace the high priest Eli and his family, who had served in the temple for generations, because Eli refused to discipline his sons, who were corrupt and using their position in the Lord's temple as a means to satisfy themselves.

In 1 Samuel 15–16, God rejects Saul as the anointed king of Israel after he refuses to be loyal to the Lord for personal gain. 1 Samuel 15:26–28 describes the judgment of Saul: "But Samuel replied, 'I will not go back with you! Since you have rejected the Lord's command, he has rejected you as king of Israel.' As Samuel turned to go, Saul tried to hold him back and tore the hem of his robe. And Samuel said to him, 'The Lord has torn the kingdom of Israel from you today and has given it to someone else—one who is better than you.'"

In the next chapter, the Lord sends Samuel out, and he anoints David as the next king of Israel. We can read about how Saul tried to regain the Lord's favor and, in failing, grew jealous of David and tried to kill him to change his circumstances. The Lord did not change His mind, and David did eventually become king instead, but the community suffered decades' worth of hardship because of Saul's choices.

These examples highlight that even though, through the Lord, all situations are redeemable and all things can be forgiven, the Lord does not spare us from the consequences of this world and our own choices. It is a *lie* that the Lord will keep you from missing out on the opportunities He has for you if you refuse to walk in obedience to Him. Some things, when they are broken or rejected, can never go back to the way they were or meant to be, at least not in this life anyway. When we are tempted to take an unhealthy risk, we need to strongly consider what we might be losing and who will bear the consequences, particularly if the things we are pursuing will be temporary.

When one person chooses to engage in unhealthy risk, usually it is the *collective* who suffer. Not taking a risk when the Lord calls you is <u>selfish</u>. Taking a risk that is not in obedience to the Lord, to pursue your wants and desires outside of Him, is <u>selfish</u>. In both scenarios, your focus is on you. Your fears, your insecurities, your wants, your needs, your comfortability. The problem is, you can't be selfish in the Kingdom of God (Matt. 20:16, Rom. 2:8, James 3:16). In 1 Corinthians, Paul describes the ways in which Jesus succeeded in living out the perfect partnership with God that Adam should have. It is not uncommon in theology for Jesus to be referenced to as the second Adam because of this, highlighting all of the ways Jesus refused to risk giving into temptations and instead took proper risks to be obedient to His purpose and calling. Where others were selfish, Jesus was selfless, so that all could be made right again.

Now that we have looked at what unhealthy risk can look like, let's go over a few questions that will help us to consider how we want to take risks.

1) Is God asking me to take a risk? And if so, what are some practical steps towards pursuing that calling?

It is **okay** to not know how to do something you have never tried or were never taught, but you shouldn't let the unknown stop you from learning. Next to nothing is truly an original concept or idea. Take the time to research your passions and invest in them with your time and resources. Reach out to other people who have had experience in that area and ask for their advice. There will be plenty of helpful tools and people willing to assist if you look for them. If God gave you the calling, He will provide what you need for it. Remember, God chooses people who say yes to the callings He gives them. If it is truly from the Lord, nothing can stop you from being able to achieve your goals except for you.

2) Who am I holding responsible for me and my life?

Maybe you have genuinely been failed by people around you who should have been more accountable and there are reasons why taking responsibility would be harder for some of us compared to others. However, no one is responsible for your choices or actions but you. If you identify with the first form of unhealthy relationship with risk where you feel like your decisions have been taken from you and you are trapped in your situation, it is your responsibility to take ownership and navigate healthy and productive ways of changing your circumstances that reflects a faith in the Lord. If you identify with the second form of unhealthy relationship with risk, where there is an impulse to explosively reset, take justice into your own hands, or put things on the line that shouldn't be risked, it is your responsibility to hold yourself accountable and discipline yourself to finding real and long-lasting solutions and walking in obedience instead of running away. There are circumstances you are facing that might not be your fault—no one chooses bad situations or hardship for themselves—but it is your responsibility to do something about it.

3) How can I get my support system involved?

Your people are your people for a reason, and they probably understand and know you better than you think. If you are too afraid to take the plunge on our own, it's okay to let them offer support and advice. They probably see things you don't see and can offer good perspectives on the situation. They will also likely appreciate the opportunity to help you achieve your goals. If you are feeling the need to be secretive and hidden from your support system, this is probably a good moment to pause and evaluate your motives and what the consequences of your actions could be if you don't involve them. Good people will not only walk all the way up a mountain with you but will also keep you from walking off the side of it.

4) What are some small steps I can take to start working towards my goals?

Maybe you hate your job and want to quit every time someone breathes at you funny. Instead of staying stagnant in the situation where you know you are miserable for a few more months or storming out in a blaze of glory, giving everyone the finger as you go, think and act towards preparing for a different future. Get your résumé together. Start asking friends and family if they know about any job openings. Look and see if it's possible to make a move within the current workplace to a different department. Pray and ask God to open doors or give you the resources and strength to create new opportunities for yourself. Start finding healthy and enjoyable ways to unwind before and after work while you wait on the Lord's timing.

There is a saying that goes, "Success is where opportunity meets preparation," and I think it is completely true. Little changes will encourage bigger changes to happen because you are open and prepared for them. There are always ways to grow and change yourself while you are waiting on external circumstances to change.

5) When I consider the consequences of this risk, and imagine those consequences happening, what am I actually risking?

There's always going to be another job, new opportunities, and other chances to try again. *Failure is a guarantee in life*, and if you are allowing the fear of risk to be dictated by temporary feelings of embarrassment, discomfort, or awkwardness, then you need to think about whether or not these are really going to be the things that you choose to be okay with holding you back. If it is replicable or replaceable, then what are you truly risking other than discomfort? On the other side of things, you need to understand when you are downplaying the risk to yourself by having the mentality that it's just one time, no one will notice, it's not a big deal, I deserve…, etc. When you have to face the repercussions of these actions or decisions, will you be okay with them? Where do you see yourself a month or a year from that decision? Will those decisions have a harmful or negative consequence for those around you?

Most of the feelings we have when we take big risks are also temporary, even if they feel bigger. Feelings of hurt, anger, pain, betrayal, fear, or an adrenaline rush are all feelings that either pass or are feelings we should eventually strive to heal from and overcome. We need to decide if the temporary relief from these feelings we might be gaining is worth potentially losing the more valuable things in our lives, things we've worked hard to build, or relationships we will not be able to get back.

6) If I took this risk, would the method and outcome be something honorable to God and myself?

None of us are strangers to instances where people have used any excuse to justify what they do or to act the way they wanted—don't be that person. Make sure you are checking your motives and meditating on whether or not you are being a representative of the Lord when you make your choices. Are my actions aligned with scripture? Do my actions show faith and reliance on the Lord? Does this action align with the person you are committed to being?

As we close out the chapter on risk, I want to leave you with these thoughts. I have never seen someone mess up so badly that God was incapable of doing anything to redeem or change the situation, and I highly doubt any of us would be the first. I don't care if you have taken risks and messed up so extraordinarily that you think there is no recovery from it. That's a lie. I don't care if you have lived out the same day for the past ten years and think that it's too late to change anything about your situation. That is a lie. Contrary to popular belief, life is actually pretty good about giving second, third, and fourth chances. And if the world is good at it, then God is *great* at it. God promises to forgive and redeem us when we surrender to Him (1 John 1:9), and He is not a liar. We can trust Him with our mustard seed, and He will move our mountains (Matt. 17:20). Do not be afraid to take the risks with Him.

Discussion Questions:

1) How would you describe your current level of comfort with risk?

_____

_____

_____

2) Do you currently have anything challenging in your life to take a risk on, and what kind of risk is it?

_____

_____

_____

_____

3) How have you dealt with risk in the past, and does it align with the type of person you want to be?

_____

_____

_____

_____

4) What are the areas in your relationship with God that need looking at if you are going to change your relationship with risk?

_____

_____

_____

_____

5) How can you tell the difference between when you are acting out of faith or obedience and selfishness?

_____

_____

_____

_____

Chapter 3
Self-Care

*"Self-care is giving the world the best of you,
instead of what's left of you."*

—Katie Reed

What comes to mind when you think of the words "self-care"? Does it conjure images of relaxing beaches, spas, beautiful escapes, and all your favorite things that indulge the senses? At the end of a long day, there is nothing I want to do more than sit down in front of a screen with my favorite foods and veg out for a few hours before bed.

Watching my favorite videos or catching up on the messages my friends sent that day is a pretty typical evening for me. When life is stressful and becomes overwhelming, the temptation to just block it all out and bury my head in the sand is strong, not only to the responsibilities overwhelming me but really to *any* responsibility.

The dishes and laundry start piling up, I'm more likely to spend money on eating out or on the things I wouldn't normally buy, or I might ignore plans with my friends and family, waving the white flag of "self-care" the whole way. When I get that free time that I've earned by ignoring other responsibilities, I continue putting off the things I need to do, and I start pouring into myself in a way that provides escape but not relief. That is usually a good indicator to me that what I'm actually doing is distracting myself, not practicing self-care.

Don't get me wrong, it's not a bad thing to take time for ourselves to do the things we want or to just turn the world off for a moment to do the silly things that don't matter, but to me, that is the difference between self-care and relaxation. Being mature means realizing that distraction and escapism won't make our lives any less stressful, and there are ways that we can practice real self-care so that when we do get a moment to relax, we can actually enjoy it and not feel overwhelmed by the laundry list that is waiting for us when we get back.

In Matthew chapter 25, Jesus tells a parable about ten bridesmaids who are waiting on the groom to show up for their friend's wedding. Five of them came prepared with the supplies they needed; the other five did not. When the groom arrived later that night, the five who were not prepared had to leave to go get the things they had neglected to bring, while everyone else started the wedding. By the time the five who were not prepared returned, they were locked out of the party and missed out.

Have you ever had a time when not being prepared came back to bite you? I can think of a few uncomfortable times I had to wear slightly damp pants to work because I had fallen behind on doing laundry and didn't run the wash through the dryer long enough before I ran out the door. Plenty of times I have either had to be hungry throughout the day or pay for more expensive meals than I normally would have because I hadn't taken the time to prepare my lunch the night before. I've procrastinated and left important things until the last minute. We all have, but when we can, it is best to be prepared.

When I am taking care of myself, I may not want to do my laundry, but I do want to be able to wear clean clothes that don't stink and aren't wet, or even have the comfort of my favorite shirt for an important occasion. I may not want to do the dishes, but I do want to be able to use the sink when I go to cook dinner tonight. Self-care looks like taking care of myself the way I would take care of someone I love. I want the people I love to eat well, to get good sleep, and to have a clean and peaceful space to come home to. When I put those things aside and choose to check out instead, half the time it's not even relaxing because I'm mentally focused on all the things I need to do anyway.

I could be watching my favorite movie or reading my favorite book, and then the thoughts will pop into my head:

"I forgot to take the trash out."
"Have I paid that bill already this month?"
"I really need to call that person back."
"Wasn't I supposed to schedule that appointment?"

I'm not able to enjoy the time I do take off, because when I finally give my mind the space it needs to breathe, the backlog of everything I have put off comes to the surface to demand my attention. Is it okay to pace ourselves when it comes to our responsibilities? **Yes.** Are most chores or errands so important that they absolutely cannot be put off until the next day? **No,** but when that's the excuse we give ourselves every day, the things we need either get put off indefinitely or are executed poorly.

Not practicing good self-care leads to feelings of inadequacy, guilt, and maybe a bit of shame. It can be embarrassing to not want to have guests over because our space is messy. It is disheartening to feel like our peers are ahead of us because of how "put together" they seem to look in comparison. These feelings don't help when everything starts piling up or we get thrown an unexpected curveball and start to become overwhelmed or burned out.

Our minds are constantly being engaged and going in a million different directions, and at times it feels like everyone, and everything, is pulling on us. Everyone seems to want our time, our energy, and our resources, and now we just don't have anything else to give because all we have been doing is draining ourselves dry instead of using our free time to fill ourselves up—if we've been making space for free time at all. It becomes extremely easy to begin putting ourselves and our care on the back burner when life happens, and it can become a case of self-neglect. We need to realize we can't pour out of an empty cup. Not for ourselves, and not for others.

We can always come up with a good excuse for why we aren't able to remember to do certain chores, why our schedule is too busy, or why doing tasks is more difficult for us compared to everyone else. If that's the case for you, good news. It sounds like you know yourself really well, and that will be a good place to start when it comes to finding ways to overcome the hang-ups.

Can't remember to take out the trash? Set an alarm. Having trouble starting chores because you think the task will take too long? The next time you go to do that task, time yourself. Most people are surprised to find that some chores really do only take five minutes. Can't find the motivation to go on a walk or get outside? Find a new podcast or make a new playlist of songs that you really want to listen to, and tell yourself that you can only listen to them while outdoors. If you know you have a problem doing something, *look for ways to get around it*. There is hardly ever just one way to do something or accomplish a goal.

If you are mistreating yourself with neglect or not being respectful of yourself, then be the one to set boundaries for yourself. Other people certainly won't do it for you. Jesus sets a great example for us here of what it looks like to practice self-care and set good boundaries. Oftentimes, after Jesus would draw a large crowd, He would retreat to a space to be alone with God (Matt. 14:23, Luke 6:12, John 6:15). Let's be honest, if it were Jesus's sole purpose to market the kingdom of heaven, then why wouldn't He just spend all day healing and performing miracles?

Surely, if a large crowd had gathered to talk to Him, He could convert even more disciples to His cause or heal a plethora of people who were suffering from terrible illnesses or ailments. However, the purpose that Jesus had wasn't to heal or convert every person He came into contact with while on this earth. If that were the case, He never would have stopped. There would still be a line, miles long, with people from every corner of the world waiting to be healed or wanting to see wonders. Jesus's purpose was to restore the relationship between God and His people, and to do that, Jesus Himself had to be in a perfect relationship with God. It was by His stripes we were healed, not His miraculous showmanship.

We cannot be in a relationship with God if we don't have the space for it because we won't take proper care of ourselves or because we don't have the time to give to the relationship. Jesus knew life would try to pressure Him and push Him into a role He wasn't meant for, so He set boundaries with Himself and others. When the crowds became too much, He walked away. When He was done speaking, He moved on to a new place. When His own disciples tried to dictate what Jesus's life should look like in a way that went against His calling or values, He would rebuke them. Jesus modeled how important partnership with God was when it came to self-care. He needed God, He knew it, and He would frequently seclude Himself for times of prayer. *God offers to share the burdens of life, not be one* (Psalm 68:19–20). So how do we begin sharing the responsibilities of life with God, and what does self-care look like in the context of having a mature relationship with God?

The Bible tells us to cast our cares onto Him (1 Pet. 5:6–7); we hear it in church all the time, but what does that mean? How do I "give everything over to God"? Let's take a look at 1 Kings chapters 18 and 19. Elijah has just finished with his big showdown with pagan worshipers where he called down the fire of God from heaven to burn logs he had soaked in water, proving that the God he served was better than the false gods everyone else had been serving and sacrificing to. He wasn't being particularly humble or respectful towards his opponents in this competition either, loudly mocking them and the gods they were attempting to persuade to send a sign.

After God answered his prayer and sent the fire down, Elijah killed many of the false prophets. Naturally, the people in power at that time did **not** enjoy this display, and Elijah was run out of town on pain of death. He wandered alone until he finally collapsed beneath a tree. While he is under this tree, Elijah declares, "I have had enough, Lord. Take my life, for I am no better than my ancestors who have already died."

Now that is a <u>statement</u>, but haven't we all done the same? Haven't we all come to a place where we are feeling alone, overwhelmed, and tired, and we tell the Lord that we've had enough? I know there have been plenty of times in my life where I've told the Lord that I wanted to quit. It is not a fun place to be. It feels exhausting in that "bone and soul tired," "everything is pointless" kind of way. It feels isolating and empty. It's usually in these moments that I personally feel like a failure, and that little worm of *doubt* starts to wiggle in. I doubt the character of God and what our relationship means to Him. So how does God respond when we come to a place where we express these negative feelings towards Him?

In Elijah's case, the first thing the Lord addressed was his physical needs. Elijah was first allowed to go to sleep and rest. An angel of the Lord even appears at least twice to bring him food and water in between the times when he is sleeping. Let's pause and take note here: **God is not oblivious to the hierarchy of needs**. He made our bodies, and He knows we need to have the basics of rest and food in order to function. There are plenty of examples in the Bible of God addressing the physical needs of the people, sometimes even before the spiritual ones. In Genesis, when Adam and Eve are naked, God clothes them. In Exodus, God provided water and manna to the Israelites as they wandered in the desert. There are also examples of Jesus doing many miracles of physical healing so that he could address the spiritual healing afterwards.

When the people were hungry, Jesus miraculously fed the multitudes who had come to hear Him speak at least twice (Mark 6:35–44, Mark 8:1–9). In Mark 2, when the disciples pick grain on the Sabbath because they are hungry, the Pharisees step in to scold them for their actions, but Jesus comes to their defense and talks about how David took food from the temple when he was hungry, even though it was unlawful. He says, "The Sabbath was made for man, not man for Sabbath." God knew our bodies needed to be fueled and rested. He cares about our physical needs enough that the Sabbath day of rest has been built in from the very beginning of time. It is hard for us to do anything when our most basic needs aren't being met. When we realize we are at a place of despair or exhaustion, let's stop and take a quick inventory of ourselves. Are my basic human needs being met?

Next, after Elijah is rested and refueled, he travels forty days and nights to have a personal council with the Lord at Mount Sinai. Forty days alone, on my way to speak to God, sounds like **a lot** of thinking and reflection time to me. Numbers are significant in the Bible, and the number forty in the Bible usually coincides with a judgment or trial. In Genesis, when God floods the earth, it rains for forty days and nights. The Israelites spent forty years in the desert before entering the promised land. Goliath taunted Saul for forty days before David came to defeat him. Jesus is tempted in the desert for forty days, and there are forty days between when Jesus was resurrected and when He ascended back into heaven. God gives Elijah time to contemplate himself before coming into His presence to receive judgment.

When we come to a place of wanting to surrender and "give it to God," we need to be aware and prepared to spend a good bit of time contemplating ourselves and realize we will need to face God's judgment as well. We also need to realize that *God's judgment isn't a bad thing*. We associate judgment with condemnation, and while judgment can be cast in that light, I feel like it forgets the form of judgment which can be defined as the ability to come to reasonable decisions or conclusions. In this instance, we are asking God for His opinion or advice on the situation, a.k.a., His judgment. We are asking God to partner with us to find a solution. However, if we are going to ask God to be our partner, we need to be ready to listen to what His opinion or advice is, even if it is different from our own or challenges our perceptions.

34

A good sign of developing maturity is having the willingness to face opinions or truths that we may not like or agree with. No one says we have to be happy about it, but we alone are incapable of seeing a situation from all perspectives the way God can. Recognizing or being willing to see our own faults and weaknesses is the first step towards overcoming them.

When Elijah makes it to the mountain and God's judgment does come, it begins in the form of a question, "What are you doing here, Elijah?" What a strange question, right? Last time I checked, Elijah was here by invitation, and God is all knowing. Why is the Lord asking him why he's here? In this case, I believe the Lord is speaking to Elijah's emotional state. In asking Elijah what he is doing here, God is not only opening up the floor for Elijah to explain his situation but also indicating that He is actively listening to how Elijah ended up in a state where he was willing to quit. God doesn't scold Elijah. He doesn't say, "You JUST called down fire from heaven and performed one of the greatest miracles of your generation that PROVED I was more powerful than any other god or force on earth! How dare you be doubtful or ungrateful?" Instead, God is patient and kind and invites Elijah into His space and gives Elijah the room to talk first and air his grievances while He listens.

Elijah speaks to the Lord and says, "I have zealously served the Lord God Almighty. But the people of Israel have broken their covenant with you, torn down your altars, and killed every one of your prophets. I am the only one left, and now they are trying to kill me, too" (1 Kings 19:10). After everything Elijah has been through and after all the time he had to think leading up to this conversation with the Lord, his complaint says a lot. What I hear in this declaration is, "I have worked hard and followed you, to the point of dying, and it wasn't enough. My actions weren't enough, my devotion wasn't enough, my faith wasn't enough. I am alone, and I am scared." In response, the Lord asks Elijah to come even closer as He puts on an impressive display of power by showing Elijah the control He has over the elements of wind, fire, and earth.

Sometimes being in the physical presence of the Lord is enough to remind us exactly how powerful He is and how small our problems truly are. What is a threat from a human compared to God, who is capable of lighting mountains on fire and throwing them around with His divine power as a flex? When we are willing to come to God in our moments of trial and doubt, God does a good job of reminding us of who He is and how much bigger He is than any problem we might be facing. *Everyone is allowed into the presence of God.* Don't be afraid to take advantage of that when you need it. In moments of self-care, it is okay to let ourselves be small and to let God be big.

Here's the thing, though. Even the reminder of who God is sometimes isn't enough to push away our doubts and fears entirely. When God asks Elijah again what he is doing here, Elijah replies with the same answer he had before. The miracle of God's first response to Elijah wasn't enough to convince him to continue on his path. God again responds to Elijah. This time He lays out His plans and tells Elijah to go back and anoint two men to be kings and another man to be a prophet. God also tells Elijah that there are seven thousand people who have not worshiped other idols. Elijah now has an action step to take and obediently goes where the Lord told him to. God gave him a task that would lead to a better future than the one he had been imagining a few verses ago when he was ready to throw in the towel.

In both of His responses to Elijah, God offers him rest, new perspectives on his situation, and invites him to think differently about his circumstances. Elijah tells God that he is working hard, and God shows Elijah how He has also been working. Elijah lets God know that he is facing big problems that are challenging, and God shows Elijah that He is bigger than the problems. Elijah tells God that he is alone in his purpose of being a prophet for God. God gives him a successor, a mission, and the encouragement that there are plenty of people who are not turned against them. For every doubt or concern Elijah had, God met him where he was to provide either an answer, perspective, or assurance, and God is capable of doing the same for us.

This is what it means to "give it to God." It means taking time to care for yourself and handle the things you can so that you can identify the things you can't or are struggling to handle. Once you have identified the points of struggle, you rest, sabbath, and take the time to present the areas of struggle to God. You can then allow the Lord to answer your problems, whether that be through prayer, scripture, changed circumstances, etc. Allow the Lord to give you a new perspective and His judgment on how to best handle the things you think you can't.

Following the example set by Elijah, when making the time for self-care by coming to God and turning our cares over to Him, think about the following questions:

1) Have my most basic human needs been met today?

Have you ever seen a small child having a public meltdown after they've gotten tired, hungry, or overstimulated? No matter how hard their parent or guardian tries, the child is not able to be comforted for a considerable period of time, no matter how much they are loved or how comforting and patient their caretaker is. We, as adults, are the same way, even if we pretend not to be. When our needs aren't being met and we hit a wall, we can close ourselves off to any sort of comfort, gentle care, or advice the Lord may be trying to give.

If we are hungry, dehydrated, tired, overwhelmed, or worked up, then we need to take a minute or two to center ourselves. Nothing is surprising to God, nor is He in a rush about anything. Unless it is a dire emergency, or you hear otherwise from the Lord, you DO have the time to go get a snack, a drink of water, do a few breathing or grounding exercises, or even take a nap before feeling like you have to address the situation right away. If we aren't taking the time to properly care for ourselves before trying to engage with God, then we shouldn't be disappointed if we don't hear anything when we weren't even in a condition to receive Him in the first place.

2) Have I taken the time to reflect on myself and my own actions, and am I open and welcoming to the judgment of God?

Sometimes life happens to us, but more often than not, life is a byprod-uct of our own actions. If we are going to ask God to partner with us in life, we need to be prepared for times when we may need to be corrected, disciplined, or shown a different perspective. There may be times where, even though we would have sworn we were right about something or acted justly, God could take this time to show us how we were wrong about something or maybe how we acted in a way that is not aligned with Him.

Are you open to being humble enough to receive correction or judg-ment? If you feel defensive about your actions or thoughts and are unwilling to share them honestly with God or feel the need to argue with God about them, it might be good to do some soul-searching to figure out *why you are so concerned with being right in your eyes versus righteous in*

God's eyes. God won't force us to be in relationship with Him. We have to be the ones to consent and submit to His advice and help and then be willing to follow through with obedience.

3) Why are you here?

When we come into the presence of the Lord, is it with purpose? Do we know what we want to talk about and why it is something we want to share with the Lord? Prayers in our modern time have fallen into a category on a checklist, but the Bible talks about praying with intention and not just to chant the same things over and over or saying things just to say them (Matt. 6:7–8). We have been granted an audience with God. On our schedule and on our conditions, we have come into His presence to speak, to ask Him to collaborate with us or to ask for His help. He opens the floor to us and is patiently listening. *So why are you here?*

4) What is God's perspective, what is His character, and am I aligning with Him?

This can be a tricky one, and it can be difficult to discern what God is like if you don't know Him. However, God makes Himself known everywhere and in everything if you are looking (Rom. 1:20). The Bible says the law is written on our hearts (Jer. 31:31–33), and all of creation reflects the glory of the Lord (Psalm 104). The longer you work on forming a strong and trusting relationship with the Lord and learning about Him through scripture and teaching, the easier it will become to discern His presence and influence. The Bible is always a good reference point as well. God can't lie or contradict Himself (Heb. 6:18), so if it isn't aligned with contextual scripture, it isn't aligned with God. God is also a living God, capable of making Himself and His will understood if we are willing to put aside our own desires and ask.

5) Am I willing to take action steps once I have my marching orders?

I don't know about you, but sometimes when I've figured out the answer to a problem, the motivation to follow through on the solution drops like a rock.

Answers from God sound appealing, but what happens when God answers us and asks us to take responsibility and put in the work to make it happen? It may seem silly to have the answers right in front of us but not act on them, but it happens a lot. There are multiple examples in the Bible as well where God gave instructions to those He had chosen, and they were resistant, hesitant, or voiced a desire to not follow through. Moses, Gideon, Jonah, Jeremiah, Abraham, and even Jesus were all asked to obey God's will when it wasn't something they wanted to do or in moments where they felt inadequate.

Following the instruction of God is hard, sometimes not what we want, or uncomfortable to a potentially painful degree. However, we need to ask ourselves what is the point in asking God for His advice if we aren't willing to take it, knowing we never had an intention to act on it? This is what it means to submit yourself to the Lord. You go before Him ready and willing to carry out His will and receive His wisdom and advice in place of your own. The point of self-care is to care for yourself well enough that when the action steps do come, you are prepared and ready to receive and act. You are called to serve, but you can only pour out to others from your own place of spiritual abundance.

6) Have I been feeling alone or isolated?

One of Elijah's chief complaints was that he was the last person to uphold the covenant between man and God. He felt alone and isolated. However, God was quick to correct Elijah in his assumption and tell him that he was not as alone as he thought. In fact there were thousands of people able to be in community with him who held his beliefs and who had also not broken covenant relationship with God. If you are feeling alone, pray and ask God to reveal where you can find support and community around you. Be prepared for the answer, though. Just because we don't feel personally surrounded by community, or maybe that the community around us isn't doing enough, doesn't mean that they aren't there or that the Lord doesn't see them too. In Elijah's case, not only was he proven wrong about his isolation, but Elijah has been traditionally tasked with bearing witness to it forever.

In Jewish ceremony, the spirit of the prophet Elijah is invited to participate in every Seder and circumcision, where he is asked to bear witness and testify for those who have continued the covenant relationship with God. "God does not permit Elijah to wallow in self-righteousness: He gives him new tasks and sends him on his way. But perhaps here, in Elijah's exaggerated condemnation of every other Jew, is the kernel of the reason for his many reappearances. He who sees himself as the last Jew is fated to bear constant witness to the eternity of Israel, to be present when every male Jewish child enters the covenant and when every Jewish family celebrates the Seder (to this day, circumcision and the Seder remain the most commonly observed Jewish rituals) Elijah stands in a long line of despairing Jews who have erroneously prophesied the end of the Jewish people."[2] *Don't give into the lie that you are alone*. Instead, intentionally seek out the truth that people and the connections you have with them that are all around you.

Discussion Questions:

1) How can I tell the difference between avoidance, relaxation, and self-care?

2) Am I currently practicing self-care in a healthy way, and how do my actions align with my answer?

_____

_____

_____

_____

3) Do I have identification and accountability systems for when I'm not practicing self-care, and what do they look like?

_____

_____

_____

_____

4) What are the current obstacles that stop me from practicing self-care, and what are my plans to overcome those obstacles in the future?

_____

_____

_____

_____

5) Am I someone who is willing to submit myself to judgment? Really think about the question before you answer, and ask yourself how often you have actually submitted to judgment in the past. (Keep in mind that receiving or hearing judgment is **NOT** the same thing as submitting to it.)

_____

_____

_____

6) Is there anything keeping me from receiving instruction from the Lord, and if so, what is it?

_____

_____

_____

_____

7) How am I stewarding my time in self-care to then be able to pour myself back out in ways that God calls me to?

_____

_____

_____

Chapter 4
Healing

*"Healing takes courage, and we all have courage,
even if we have to dig a little to find it."*
—Tori Amos

Healing can be a touchy subject for a lot of people for a lot of good reasons, whether it is spiritual healing, emotional healing, or physical healing. It is exceedingly rare to find anyone who has not suffered some kind of major setback or trauma in their lives that affects how they see the world and interact with it. Once we become adults, it is important to acknowledge that the difficult or bad things we lived through might not have been our fault, but it is our responsibility to look at the trials we have faced so far in life and observe whether or not they have been processed and dealt with in a healthy way.

Since becoming an adult, I have noticed that because these hardships are such significant and defining moments in our lives, it is easy and even sometimes encouraged for these hurts to become a source of identity. I think one problem with linking our identities to our illnesses, hurts, or traumas is that, if we believe the Bible, these are all temporary states of being and not a good foundation to build our lives upon. Another potential problem with putting our hurts at the center of our identities is that it makes us resistant to finding healing and developing healthier outlooks and connections. We need to take notice of how the lack of healing affects our ability to handle conflict, accept responsibilities, have difficult conversations, interact in relationships, face rejection, or react to criticism. Is there a feeling of anger, fear, resentment, defensiveness, dismissiveness, or dread? These things can keep us from growing and advancing in life towards the self we are trying to become.

Do not take this as an invitation or call to bury the negative under the cover of religion. If you have ever heard someone say or if you yourself have felt the need to cover up the dark, shameful, or hurtful parts of you for the sake of Jesus or the reputation of the church, then I need you to hear me now: ***that is a lie and does not align with scripture in any way***. In the Kingdom of God there are no closets to hide the skeletons in (Heb. 4:13, Luke 8:17, Matt. 10:26–28). The relationship we have with God is meant to bring the darkness to light to heal it, not hide it further (Isa. 42:16). There is a healthy medium where we can acknowledge, heal, or sometimes repent from our past, hurts, and struggles while at the same time not letting them control us or dictate our future. The Bible says and observes that we are broken people (it wasn't a secret), but Jesus died to offer us a new identity in Christ and not one based on the hurts of this world and the sins we have committed or the sins that have been committed against us (Psalm 103:8–14, 2 Cor. 5:17). Why should you or I surrender any more of our lives to the things that hold us back when we could surrender to God instead?

Healing is painful, and it takes strength to investigate hurts, but we DO have that strength, and we CAN do hard things to move towards doing better for our future.

Healing is not our enemy. The Bible says Jesus came that we may have life and have it abundantly (John 10:10). I think we all deserve to know that we are capable of living a life where we are able to let go of our struggles and find peace from the things that have hurt or defined us in the past. This particular path of growth is often uncomfortable, exposing, and maybe even heartbreaking at times. However, maybe it is better to suffer some uncomfortable moments now than face a lifetime of carrying burdens around that we didn't need to because we refused to address our hurts.

I want to make one thing very clear upfront before we dive deeper into the chapter on healing. While I do believe that knowing and learning about the character and will of God through prayer and scripture is an invaluable and <u>powerful</u> tool when it comes to the healing process, it is but one tool in a toolbox full of resources. Do not treat every problem like it can be solved using only one method. This is an inaccurate assumption and a waste of time for everyone involved. If you believe you need or want professional or medical help to face your individual struggles, then you need to seek it out, knowing your worth and knowing that God will be with you through that process.

It is, unfortunately, not uncommon to have to go to multiple doctors' appointments to nail down a medical issue, and it's not uncommon to seek out multiple counselors or therapists before you find one that you are comfortable with. If you have not received the care you think you need, advocate for yourself and keep looking, even if it is tiresome and frustrating, until you get the help you are looking for. Pray and ask God for healing, <u>always</u>, but also ask God to advocate for you and to help you find the right person who will listen, provide the resources you need, or to give a doctor the wisdom and discernment needed to see the problems you are facing. With that in mind, let's take a look at some characteristics of healing in the Bible.

If we are being honest, the Bible is about the furthest thing from the warm and fuzzy, sunshine and rainbows book it is sometimes claimed to be. It is FULL of real human beings who are, quite frankly, the most broken and messed up people we can imagine. Plenty of people in the Bible deal with anxiety, depression, doubt, and trauma and are crime victims and face nearly every negative human experience we can imagine on this earth. The people in the Bible are also murderers, thieves, and outcasts with selfish, condescending, judgmental, and lying characters, and usually these are the people we are supposed to be rooting for.

However, the broken places where we find these figures in the Bible aren't typically where God leaves them. God steps in and takes the selfish, lying murderers and radically transforms them into the leaders of nations. God goes out of His way to find the broken outcasts nobody would have chosen and gives them a place in the narrative anyway. God takes the people who are only known for their ailments and gives them new identities. Even though healing looks different for everyone, here are a few common threads I have found in stories of healing in scripture.

One of the first major things I've noticed is that the people who receive healing in the Bible typically fall into one of two categories. The first group are the ones who were already seeking healing in the world and ultimately find God while they are searching for it. The second group are the ones who are not seeking help or expecting God to heal them, but who are approached by the Lord regardless and offered healing if they are willing to accept it.

It is astounding to me how often the Lord will ask for permission in the way of waiting until someone approaches or submits to His help before the healing is able to take place. *Healing is always done in partnership.*

There are plenty of examples of physical healing in the ministry of Jesus. One example is the miracle of the woman with the bleeding issue documented in Matthew 9. The woman had faced this same bleeding issue for over a decade and had gone to many different spiritual leaders and doctors looking for help and answers but had not been able to find any. When she hears the Messiah is coming, she has faith and seeks Him out. She is not healed until she touches the cloak of Jesus, and the Scripture makes it clear she had to fight through a crowd of people to do so. She had not given up on her healing, even after twelve years of disappointment and failure.

The crippled man at Bethesda in John 5 had been at the well for thirty-eight years when Jesus approached him to ask, "Do you want to be healed?" The chapter says that there were plenty of people waiting to be healed at this pool, but Jesus seeks out this man specifically. When the man indicates he does want healing, Jesus doesn't snap His fingers and say, "You're healed!" Jesus instead tells the man to get up and walk, inviting him to literally take an action step of faith.

In John chapter 9, Jesus encounters a man who is born blind. People ask Jesus if the man or his parents had sinned for him to have been afflicted with blindness. Jesus replies that neither is the case and that the man was born blind so that the work of God might be displayed in him. Jesus rubs mud in the man's eyes and tells him to go wash in the pool at Siloam. After following Jesus's instructions, the man is able to see for the first time in his life.

There are examples of God working to heal emotional and spiritual wounds as well. In Genesis chapter 16, Hagar is forced by Sarai to sleep with Abram because he and Sarai are struggling to get pregnant even after the Lord had promised them a son of their own. When Hagar does become pregnant, the Bible says she begins to despise her mistress, and Sarai ends up mistreating Hagar so badly that she runs away. The Lord seeks out Hagar alone and asks her, "Where have you come from and where are you going?"

The Lord approaches Hagar, the runaway Egyptian slave who may or may not even believe in Him, to hear about the wrongs that had been done to her. The Lord isn't giving Abram and Sarai a free pass and turning a blind eye to their mistreatment of both Hagar and the promise He gave them to have their own children. Instead, He gives Hagar the room to speak to Him, and after hearing her predicament, He asks her to go back and submit to Sarai anyway, *but before she does*, God gives her the following promises: God promises her that she will have descendants that are too numerous to count. He promises her a son and tells her to name him Ishmael, which means "God hears." He lastly promises her that Ishmael will live in hostility with his relatives. Hagar in turn gives God the name "El Roi" or "the God who sees me." Hagar does go back to submit to Sarai as the Lord asked, and when Hagar and Ishmael are eventually exiled, the Lord again comes to their aid and promises to build a great nation from the line of Ishmael. Ishmael does go on to become a leader of nations and is in fact considered to be one of the patriarchs of Islam.

Another example of emotional healing is the story of Hannah, the mother of Samuel. In 1 Samuel 1, Hannah goes to the temple and pours out her heart to God after she has been childless and bullied for years. She offers to submit her child to the service of the Lord if He will give her a son. She was so bitter and sad in her prayers that the temple priest actually thought she was drunk. After praying to the Lord, Scripture doesn't say that Hannah left with a guarantee that the Lord would answer the prayer, but it does say when she walked away from the temple, she no longer felt sad. The Lord does grant Hannah's request for a child, and true to her word, she dedicated Samuel's life to the temple.

In both the physical and emotional instances of healing, *there is a call to submit to the Lord in one way or another,* either by showing a desire to be healed by the undeniable power of the Lord or by agreeing to submit to His will. There is an action step each person has to take that indicates their own free will and intention to partner with God: the woman has to fight the crowd to touch Jesus, the man at the well has to stand up and walk, the blind man has to go wash his eyes out, Hagar had to go back to Sarai, and Hannah had to give her son back into the service of the Lord.

In each of the above examples, there is another gift offered in healing: a new identity. Do we ever notice how often in the Bible, particularly in the New Testament, when a miracle of physical healing is performed, the person healed is not always named? I don't imagine it would have been hard to ask their names. There are other people referenced by name to be witnesses in the gospel. Why not give the name of the person that was healed so that they could be witnesses too? The most likely reason I can think of is because the people around town would have known the person by their ailments and not by their name. I imagine the conversation would have gone something like this: "Hey, did you hear Jesus healed Jerry yesterday? You know, Jerry! No? He was the crippled guy who sat by the well for thirty-eight years!"

That's the thing: after the healings, they could no longer have the identities of the bleeding woman, the cripple, the blind man, the slave, or the childless woman, <u>because they weren't anymore</u>.

Pause here and read John chapter 9 in its entirety. After the blind man is healed, the local Pharisees cannot believe the healing and call not only the blind man to testify but his parents as well. They accuse the blind man of having lied about his blindness or having stolen the identity of a blind man to claim a false miracle happened. He is transformed so completely that his identity *literally* cannot be believed. After being repeatedly interrogated, the once-blind man hears the Pharisees accusing Jesus of being a sinner and a liar. He interjects and says, "Whether he is a sinner or not, I don't know. One thing I do know. I was blind but now I see." They asked him again how Jesus healed him, and he said, "I have told you already and you did not listen. Why do you want to hear it again? Do you want to become His disciples too?" After the Pharisees kick him out of their court, Jesus finds the man later and offers him salvation, showing how the physical healing was just the first step in paving the way for spiritual reconciliation and relationship.

In the case of Hagar, she was a slave, removed from her homeland, assaulted, mistreated, abused, and abandoned, but the one who comes looking for her is the Lord. He shows her respect, gives her a new identity and purpose in the midst of her hardship, and makes her the mother of a nation. Hannah was a bitter wife, scorned and childless. She became the mother of the prophet who brought about the age of kings for the Israelites. God is interested in healing the whole person, not just the ailments. The changes are drastic, but He gives each of them a new identity that is secure and undeniable, with a foundation in faith and action.

The next biggest thing I have noticed as a consistency with healing in scripture is the importance of the community we surround ourselves with. *Community matters in healing.* In 2 Kings 5, Namaan is a mighty warrior who suffers from a skin disease. After finding no one able to cure his ailment in his own country, a slave girl informs her master that there is someone, the prophet of the Lord, Elisha, who will be able to help him. The Bible describes Namaan traveling from the kingdom of Aram to the kingdom of Israel along with an entourage, their horses, and chariots to find healing for the incurable disease. He offered clothes, silver, and gold as payment.

When he came to the home of Elisha, the prophet refused to meet with Namaan face-to-face and instead sent a messenger to instruct Namaan to bathe in the Jordan River seven times to be healed. The mighty and wealthy warrior, feeling insulted at being denied an audience, stalks away and is prepared to leave, but the officers who were with him convinced Namaan to bathe in the river anyway. When he emerges from the river healed, Namaan declares the Lord to be the one true God.

In Mark 2, there is a paralyzed man who is healed after his friends brought him to Jesus by lowering him down through the roof of the building that Jesus was teaching in. The Scripture says that Jesus was moved by their faith. In John 4, Jesus heals an official's son after the father comes and asks for healing on his child's behalf. In Luke 7, Jesus resurrects the only son of a widow after He sees her crying and has compassion for her.

In Matthew 8, a centurion comes to Jesus and asks him to heal his servant, who was sick, acknowledging that if Jesus would only speak the command, his servant would be healed. The man impresses Jesus with his faith and understanding of authority. Jesus says to him, "Assuredly, I say to you, I have not found such great faith, not even in Israel! [...] Go your way; as you have believed, so let it be done for you." The faith of others isn't going to grant us salvation, but the way our communities can intercede for us and uplift us is acknowledged by God and holds power.

A strong support system can help provide not just for our daily needs (Acts 2:42–47), but they can also help carry our burdens (Gal. 6:2) and love us through difficult times (Prov. 17:17). *We are made to be in community with each other.* We are built for it, and we have a better chance of healing and overcoming any obstacle if we surround ourselves with the right people. Ecclesiastes 4 says, "Two people are better off than one, for they can help each other succeed. If one person falls, the other can reach out and help. But someone who falls alone is in real trouble. Likewise, two people lying close together can keep each other warm. But how can we be warm alone? A person standing alone can be attacked and defeated, but two can stand back-to-back and conquer. Three are even better, for a triple-braided cord is not easily broken."

Just as a good community can be a boost to our healing, an unhealthy community can have the opposite effect and be harmful to us. We may love our friends and family, but sometimes it can be hard to see how they can pull us away from goodness, wisdom, and healing, both intentionally and unintentionally. In 1 Kings chapter 12, there is a story about the young king Rehoboam. The people of Israel came to Rehoboam at the beginning of his reign and told him that his father, the previous king Solomon, had given them a heavy yoke and harsh labor, but if Rehoboam were to lighten the burdens of the people, they would serve him. Rehoboam asks them to give him three days to decide on their request.

He first seeks advice from the elders, who had served for many years as counselors to the royals. They recommended that he serve his people and show them favor, and they believed that if he did the people would serve him in return. However, Rehoboam rejects the elder's advice and then goes to the young men who had grown up with him to ask their advice. They counsel him to be even harsher than his father was to the people and demand even more of them. Rehoboam takes the advice of his friends over the wise counsel of the elders, and as a result, Israel rebels against him, and the kingdom of Israel is divided between Rehoboam and a new king Jeroboam. In 1 Kings 14, it says that the armies of Rehoboam and Jeroboam stayed at war with each other until Rehoboam's death.

Rehoboam trusted his friends, and his friends gave him the advice that he wanted to hear, not the advice that was wise. The decision to act, the responsibility of the situation, and the consequences ultimately fall on Rehoboam, but the influence of his friends clearly led him down a path of destruction for his country instead of stability or healing for the people who had already been suffering under the rule of the previous king.

In Judges 16, Samson, a great warrior who had favor with the Lord, falls in love with Delilah, and she uses the love that he has for her to manipulate him into telling her the secrets of his supernatural strength. Multiple times she tries to trick him into revealing the truth about his strength, but he lies to her about it until his soul was vexed to death. Finally, he tells her that if his hair was cut, his strength would leave him. There are clear signs of manipulation and unhealthy boundaries on both sides of the relationship. Samson and Delilah both lie repeatedly to each other and try to manipulate each other to get what they want. When Samson did finally reveal his very literal vulnerabilities to Delilah, she betrayed him.

In the KJV Bible, it says, "And when Delilah saw that he had told her all his heart, she sent and called for the lords of the Philistines, saying, 'Come up this once, for he hath shewed me all his heart.'" Other translations of the Bible say, "He has told me the truth," but I think in this instance I personally prefer the phrase, "He showed me his heart," because it's true. Delilah made Samson believe she loved him and told him that if he loved her too, he would share his secrets, long after she had proven herself to be an unsafe person to him. As a result of continuing in an unhealthy and untrustworthy relationship, Samson has his eyes gouged out, he is taken prisoner, and he is chained and put on display at a party of his enemies who are rejoicing over his defeat.

Maybe the consequences of trusting the wrong people won't be quite as severe as what Samson and Rehoboam faced, but we need to be careful about who we let into our lives and understand the very real ways that surrounding ourselves with the wrong people will only hurt us, not help us. A lot of emotional and spiritual wounds stem from wanting to be loved and valued by the people closest to us in our lives. There are people who will use the desire for validation or the wounds we have as a tool to manipulate and control us to satisfy or fill something within themselves. Sometimes they don't even realize that's what they are doing, but we are the ones who end up with the consequences of it.

It is hard to control someone who feels whole, loved, and knows their worth. We should want to surround ourselves with people who we can trust and who uplift us, because healing is difficult and time consuming. We need to trust that when we go through the vulnerable process of healing, we feel safe and secure with the people who walk with us through those trials and changes. People who will challenge us to pursue the things we need and not just the things we want.

God walks with us through the hard times of healing as well. As we talked about earlier, God is in the business of healing the whole person, not just the symptoms, and that takes time. The Bible says God is patient, gentle, and kind, especially with our hurts. Psalm 34 says, "The Lord hears His people when they call to Him for help. He rescues them from all their troubles. The Lord is close to the brokenhearted; He rescues those whose spirits are crushed. The righteous person faces many troubles, but the Lord comes to the rescue each time."

To be clear, not everyone receives healing in the way they expect it or the help they want from the Lord when they need it (Luke 4:25–27). Sometimes the needs or hurts we have are never met in a way that satisfies us. Sometimes physical ailments, mental illnesses, and diseases aren't taken away, even when we pray for them to be. *However, that doesn't mean that God doesn't see or that He doesn't care.*

In Genesis 29, Jacob has two wives. He clearly shows love and favoritism to his second wife, Rachel, while outright emotionally neglecting his first wife, Leah. The scriptures make it clear Leah is hurt deeply by this and that it is her greatest desire to be loved by her husband. Jacob never shows her the love and affection she wanted from him, and the hurts she suffers as an unloved wife are never rectified in their relationship. However, the Lord acknowledges and shows favor to Leah and gives her many children instead, including the son that will be a direct ancestor to Jesus. Leah may have never had a healed and healthy relationship with her husband, but that didn't mean that the Lord didn't bless her and show her love in other ways.

In 2 Corinthians 12, Paul says he was afflicted with an ailment of some kind that he calls "a thorn in my flesh." Whatever problems this "thorn" causes are not explicitly described, but Paul does say, "Three different times I begged the Lord to take it away. Each time He said, 'My grace is all you need. My power works best in weakness.' So now I am glad to boast about my weakness, so that the power of Christ can work through me."

Some of the most powerful testimonies I have ever heard have come from people who have overcome and found healing through some of the worst imaginable trials of this life. God doesn't promise to cure cancer, chronic health issues, or mental illness, but He does promise to help us through these things (John 16:33). God does not abandon us to this world and its hurts or discount us because of our afflictions. What isn't healed in this world will eventually be set right. That's what Jesus died for. Revelation 21 says, "Look, God's home is now among His people! He will live with them, and they will be His people. God Himself will be with them. He will wipe every tear from their eyes and there will be no more death or sorrow or crying or pain. All these things are gone forever."

We are not valued more or less by God as broken people, but that doesn't mean that we want to live our lives as broken people and that we can't take steps to pursue healing while we are still on earth.

So, when it comes to pursuing health (physical, mental, emotional, or spiritual), what are some questions we can ask ourselves to get started?

1) Am I resistant to healing, and if so, why?

Particularly when it comes to emotional and spiritual healing, it can be hard to let go of the hurts that keep us stuck because they are harder to see and can be harder to investigate. Most of the wounds related to healing also have a root in wanting fairness or justice, and it can be difficult to see our feelings around these topics as obstacles to our healing when they feel like the solution to it.

"If I let go of my anger towards someone, then there will be no one to hold them accountable for the bad things they did to me." But do I want to live my life as an angry person if the justice I seek never comes in this lifetime? *"I am afraid to reach out for help because I have been rejected before."* But do I want to remain afraid or not receive the help I need? *"I am not the problem; they are."* Maybe they are, but am I going to let pride keep me from addressing the hurt they caused because I'm waiting for them to decide to take responsibility for their faults, but <u>what if they never do</u>? Where does that leave you?

Feelings tend to fester. The longer they go unaddressed, the more deeply they can become ingrained into our personality and identity. It can be hard to let go of something that has motivated you or defined you for so long, but is the end result of letting the hurt control you going to lead to the type of person you want to be for yourself and for others you love?

2) What action steps am I willing to take to find healing in a healthy way?

Health is an investment. I know it can be hard to justify spending time and money on ourselves over the things that we feel are small problems now or over things we have decided we can live with, but what if one day those small problems become bigger problems and we don't want to live with them anymore? Are you willing to wait for months to get set up with the right doctors? Are you willing to try counseling or therapy even if there's a stigma around it? Are you willing to change lifestyles or break habits if you can recognize that they are weighing you down?

3) Am I in an environment that will help me succeed in my goals?

Nothing will grow in the wrong conditions. Are you in an environment where you feel safe and secure? Do you feel like you surround yourself with the kind of people who can support you and encourage you to advance in life? Can you trust your community to help you set boundaries and hold you accountable to living a healthy life? Do you feel like you can be completely honest and transparent with at least a few people in your life, even about the hardest or darkest things, who will lovingly point you back to Christ and your goals when you are struggling? Are you regularly providing yourself with or receiving the care you need? Are there accommodations or changes that can be made to your environment that would make things easier for you?

4) What are the consequences I have seen others face as a result of not seeking out healing?

I think we can all be honest and say that a majority of us have been hurt at some point by someone in our lives who, if we sat them down and confronted them about the hurts they have done, would not take responsibility in a way that is satisfying to us. They might instead list off all the reasons why they weren't able to provide what we needed from them. Depending on how self-focused they were, they may not even realize that we suffered as a result of their actions or choices. They might even deny the moments that hurt us even happened at all if they are set on rejecting the idea that they would be in the wrong. I don't know about you, but none of the excuses, even when I can understand them, ever feel justified for the hurts suffered.

Now, just for a moment, picture yourself and your traumas and hurts in the future if you continue to carry them around with you. Will you one day have someone you love sitting across from you, telling you about all the ways you failed or hurt them as a result? Will the excuses given now be enough of a justification to not have taken responsibility to seek out help and healing when you had the chance to prevent this cycle from continuing to happen?

There's the old saying, "Hurt people hurt people." When this happens within the family structure, this is what some people define as generational curses. Until someone in the chain is willing to put in the work to make it stop, <u>it won't</u>.

5) How much of my identity have I based on my traumas or hurts?

Think of some of your most defining characteristics or biggest motivators when it comes to decision-making. What lens are you seeing the world through? Are my hurts, traumas, or shortcomings a focal point for my thoughts, conversations, or interactions? Do I isolate myself exclusively with people who have had similar experiences as me and reject others because I believe they won't have compassion or understanding? Do I feel like if I were to pursue healing, it would be a rejection or betrayal of myself or pull me away from the connections I have formed within my community? Do I set goals for myself with the intention of "proving them wrong" or to build up barriers around myself so "they can't hurt me anymore"? What are the three biggest core memories that have shaped me into who I am today?

6) What do I believe about God and His role in the afflictions I have that need healing?

Maybe you struggle with feelings or thoughts where you blame God for your current circumstances. Maybe you think your "thorns" or your ailments are punishments from God or a test of your faithfulness. How do you reconcile a good God with the reality of your hurts? <u>That is a reasonable question to ask</u>. The same way Paul prayed to God multiple times to ask for an explanation, don't be afraid to do the same. As we have discussed before, God is a living God capable of making Himself known and understood if you come to Him seeking knowledge and understanding. Pray and ask Him for the answers you need. Just be careful that when you pray you haven't already decided on your answer or passed your judgment on Him before you ever asked.

Discussion Questions:

1) How are you partnering with God when it comes to your healing?

_____

_____

_____

_____

2) What are some of the benefits you have been able to experience from finding healing?

_____

_____

_____

_____

3) What resources are you currently investing into your health?

4) Do you currently have any restrictions you put on yourself when it comes to healing, and if so, what are they?

5) How much of your current identity is based on things you don't feel healed from?

6) How would changing your environment or circumstances aid in your healing process, and what are the practical steps or goals you can set to develop that atmosphere?

_____

_____

_____

_____

7) How are you being supported when it comes to your health?

_____

_____

_____

_____

8) Do you believe God is interested in inflicting pain and suffering on you instead of helping to heal you, and what makes you think that?

_____

_____

_____

_____

Chapter 5
Self-Worth

"Value is what people are willing to pay for it."
—John Naisbitt

So, here's the thing: we are going to have to live with ourselves and keep our own company for our entire lives. Outside of God, no one is going to be closer to us than we are to ourselves, yet it is amazing to me how little we know about ourselves and how little we sometimes value ourselves. I firmly believe that if you don't learn to have a grasp on your own self-worth, you will never be able to properly value anything else in life. Think of the most expensive things in this world or the most precious resources. Do you realize that between God and the enemy described as Satan, neither of them has ever wasted even a single second fighting over or trying to obtain any of those things? *The only thing God has ever cared about or put any value or worth on is you and your relationship with Him, and the only thing the enemy has ever cared about was making sure you don't believe it.*

It can be hard to feel like we are the most valuable thing to God when we struggle to value ourselves. I think we are really good at "knowing" truths about God based on things we have learned or been told but not **KNOWING** that truth as an unshakable belief and foundation that we build our lives upon. In the past, we may not have been encouraged to question God or teachings about Him when His promises don't feel true. For example:

"I know the Bible says God loves me; there's a song about it and everything, but I don't feel loved when life comes along and puts me on my butt. I feel beaten down and worthless."

The Bible says that our hearts are deceitful (Jer. 17:9), but we can allow them to steward our lives more than we might care to admit. All feelings are valuable, but all feelings are meant to be temporary. Feelings are indicators of our current state of being, and they shouldn't be ignored, *but they are not a universal or permanent truth*. However, isn't it amazing how much we tie our own value directly to how loved or appreciated we feel by our parents, partners, friends, mentors, or coworkers?

The sad reality is, maybe those figures in your life *don't* value you as they should. On the other hand, any one or all of these people could tell you and show you that they love, appreciate, and support you every day, but not a single one of them can make you believe or receive that you are valued *if you don't think it's true*. Not to mention, no one is capable of loving you perfectly. I think an immature line of thinking, and a lie that is sold to us in modern culture, is that other people or things are capable of loving us or fulfilling us in the way we need to feel whole. Whether that love comes from a significant other, a parent, a child, or a friend really doesn't matter, but when imperfect love does fall short, that failure is often internalized and used as a tool to make us doubt our own worthiness.

I find that when I investigate the root of a lot of my doubts and insecurities about my worth to myself and to God, at the center is a lie that I have come to believe about my identity or about God. There is a tiny voice in everyone's head that loves to lie and lies in a way that sounds **A LOT** like the truth. In fact, the lie is usually based on the truth but pushed, as I would like to say, *"a little to the left."* For example, I think all of us can think back to something that we said or did that was wrong or embarrassing. That little voice likes to tell us:

"You are embarrassing."
"You are an idiot."
"This is the thing people remember about you and what you are known for."

There may be a little bit of truth to those memories—maybe I *did* do something stupid, maybe I *did* do something cringy or embarrassing, maybe people *do* remember it—but an act of stupidity doesn't make me stupid, and a moment of embarrassment doesn't make me an embarrassing person. I can change out a spent lightbulb in my apartment, but that doesn't make me an electrician. It's only when I put my flaws at the core of my beliefs about myself that I make those choices repeatedly, and eventually it does become a part of my identity. This is what we might call a self-fulfilling prophecy. You believe these flaws are true parts of who you are, so eventually that is what you build the foundation for your identity on even if the beliefs about yourself are false. However, when you have a firm grasp on your true identity and worth, it is a lot harder to try to claim something else in its place.

So how do you find and get a good grip on your identity in Christ? What does "having an identity in Christ" mean? The first place you can turn to is scripture. Take a look at this below and tell yourself the phrase, "In Christ, I am (insert word/phrase below)." Does that statement feel true, or does it feel like a lie?

A Child of God (John 1:12)	Forgiven (Col. 1:14)
Given Hope (Eph. 1:12)	Protected (John 10:28–29)
Loved (Rom. 5:8)	Granted Mercy (Eph. 2:4–5)
Rejoiced over (Zeph. 3:17)	A Friend of Jesus (John 15:15)
Strong (2 Cor. 12:9–11)	Free (Gal. 5:1)
Complete (Col. 2:10)	More than a Conqueror (Rom. 8:37)
An Heir (Rom. 8:16–17)	Offered Peace (Phil. 4:7)
Given Power (Luke 10:17–20)	Not Abandoned (John 14:18)
Not Condemned (Rom. 8:1)	Capable (Phil. 4:11–13)
Provided for (Matt. 6:25–34)	Not an Accident (Eph. 2:10)
Understood (Heb. 4:15–16)	Changed (Rom. 12:2)
Saved by Grace (Eph. 2:8–9)	Cherished (Isa. 43:4)

If you believe scripture cannot lie, then when you come across a statement that doesn't feel true about you or your life circumstances, take some time to think about why you think or believe the scripture is wrong. Next take your "whys" to God in prayer and ask Him to reveal the truth of that belief to you.

Likewise, it is hard to feel the truth of God's love for you if you are believing lies about Him. Look over this list and tell yourself the phrase: God is (insert one of the characteristics below). Do any of these character traits feel false or untrue when you think about your current perception of God?

Love (1 John 4:16)	A Sure Foundation (Isa. 28:16)
A Deliverer (Col. 1:13)	A Miracle Worker (Gal. 3:5)
Faithful and True (Rev. 19:11)	A Redeemer (Gal. 3:13)
All-Powerful (Jer. 32:17)	Relatable and Empathetic (Heb. 4:15)
A Servant (Mark 10:45)	Unchangeable (Num. 23:19)
Steadfast (Heb. 13:5)	Humble (Phil. 1:6–8)
All-Knowing (1 John 3:20)	Dwelling Within Us (2 Cor. 6:16)
Sacrificial (Rom. 5:8)	A Father and Counsellor (Isa. 9:6)
A Healer (Isa. 53:5)	A Warrior (Exd. 15:3)
Mighty to Save (Isa. 63:1)	A Teacher (Psalm 32:8)
Good (1 Chr. 16:34)	Provider of Needs (Phil. 4:19)
An Advocate (1 John 2:1)	Wise (Jer. 10:12)
A High Priest (Heb. 9:11)	The Light of the World (John 8:12)

Intimate (Psalm 139:1–4)	Head of the Church (Eph. 1:22)
Happy to Share His Kingdom (Luke 12:32)	Maker of Beautiful Things (Eccl. 3:11)
All-Sufficient (2 Cor. 3:5)	Kind and Merciful (Titus 3:4–6)
Worthy of Praise (Psalm 18:3)	

Really take a minute and think about these lists, or feel free to insert any other characteristic here that can be verified contextually by scripture.

I personally don't care in this particular moment what you may know about what the Bible says or what you may have heard a preacher say from the pulpit on a Sunday. _Perception is reality_. If you feel that any of these things are untrue when you say them out loud, then odds are you are operating from a frame of mind that accepts that either the God we have been told about is a lie or that, if He is real, then He is a liar. That might not be something anyone wants to share out loud or maybe even admit to themselves, but let me say that it is okay to have doubts as long as you are willing to confront them appropriately.

So how do you confront doubts about God's character or about your own worth? First things first, start to teach yourself how to identify when things you are being told about God or your worth are _"a little to the left."_ If you look at the example of Adam and Eve in Genesis, the serpent that visits them does a good job of using questions to cast doubt into their minds about whether or not God really cares about them. There are phrases used like, "Did God really say... surely not...." The serpent in the story even implies that the reason God won't let Adam and Eve eat the fruit of the tree is because God is withholding power and wisdom from them because God doesn't want man to be like Him. In that moment, their attention wasn't on literally everything else in the garden God had given them; it was on the one thing they were being told He hadn't. They are asked to question if God was being truthful or if He was keeping good things from them.

What is ironic about the situation is that the serpent is tempting them _with something they already have_. The serpent promises that eating from the tree of the knowledge of good and evil will make them like God (Gen. 3:5). Yet, if you go back a few verses, God Himself says that He made man in His own image to rule over the things of the Earth (Gen. 1:26). They were already like God.

True, they may have been lacking in the knowledge of good and evil department, but they had a close enough relationship with God to ask Him anything they wanted to know. Yet they allowed themselves to be tempted away from the truth into a place of doubt over something they already were or had. I have often imagined how differently this scenario would have gone if either Adam or Eve had said, "You know what, these are some good questions you have brought up, and I feel unsure. I'm going to go reflect on these thoughts and maybe ask God when we are walking together later this evening."

Very rarely in scripture does God completely reject questions or doubts when they are brought to light from a place of seeking understanding. Moses comes up with every excuse under the sun for why he shouldn't be chosen to lead the Israelites, and God is patient to answer the doubts and chooses Moses anyway (Exod. 3:11–4:17). Abraham questions God about the decision to destroy Sodom and Gomorrah (Gen. 18:20–33), and God is open and accepts the arguments and conditions that Abraham gives when it comes to sparing the city—not once, not twice, but six times! When Habakkuk questioned God on the wall, God was patient enough to listen and answer his concerns (Hab. 1–2). When Jesus was praying before the crucifixion, He prayed that, if it was possible, God would remove the burden of the cross from Him, even though He ultimately submitted to the will of God in the end (Matt. 26:39).

The point being, there are verses that talk about not testing God, but there is scriptural evidence to show that it is okay to ask God questions, and there is room to grapple with our doubts and fears *with* Him. In James 1:5, the Bible says, "If any of you lacks wisdom, you should ask God, who gives generously to all without finding fault, and it will be given to you." God is a **living** God, perfectly capable of revealing Himself and representing Himself to you. If you have doubts about Him or about the value He assigns to you, just ask Him directly.

Another way to go about investigating your worth to God when you don't feel it is to look at scripture. Do me a quick favor and pause here to go read some, if not all, of the following verses:

Matthew 10:29–30	Hebrews 4:12–16
Psalm 139	Deuteronomy 7:6–9
Matthew 6:25–34	Ephesians 2:4–9
Luke 12:6–7	Psalm 8
Romans 5:6–8	

One thing I selfishly love about God is that He values us before we have ever done anything to earn or deserve it. *God is not like everyone else*; He doesn't wait until we have proven ourselves worth His time. He doesn't wait until we love Him back, do something impressive, or say the right things. Before you or I were even capable of walking, speaking, caring, or thinking, God was and had invested in us. Not for what we can do for Him, but because of who we are to Him.

Another place to revisit when you are doubting your value to God is your own memories and experiences with Him. God is consistent, can't lie, and can't change His character (2 Tim. 2:13). If the Bible claims that He is loving, good, and cares about you right now, then you should have a lifetime of evidence proving that it's true. The world and the people in it might not have treated you well or valued you all the time, but from the beginning, God hasn't been in the habit of controlling others. God doesn't take away anyone's choice to sin or to choose the things that are harmful to us or themselves; *that doesn't mean He agrees with them or condones their actions either.* In fact, He promises discipline and retribution for those who choose their own path of sin, hate, and destruction over living a life of goodness like the Lord intended (Psalm 37, Jer. 12).

Another benefit of having a real grasp on what your worth is, is that you can also more accurately assess other people's worth. The same way we talked about not allowing isolated actions or moments to dictate our identity earlier, we are better able to see that the same principle applies to the people around us. People aren't necessarily just mean and hateful to be mean and hateful. They act in mean and hateful ways because of their own hurt and their own lack of understanding of their own worth and the worth of those around them. The kingdom God offers is one of abundance and assurance, not competition and doubt. No one has to doubt or compete for God's love and attention; *they already have it.*

I have heard the Kingdom of God described as a huge, never-ending buffet table of the best food available, with an open invitation for anyone who wants to eat. When I genuinely believe and see that there is plenty of food for everyone, I'm probably not going to be all that concerned if someone cuts in line ahead of me or if someone takes the last cookie from the plate if I know another overflowing tray is coming along in the next two minutes. Most of the time, people aren't against you; they are just for themselves, and when you don't understand your worth, you can be tempted to refocus your life to be about you.

People who reorient their lives to be about themselves in an unhealthy or obsessive way usually inflict pain on those around them to maintain that focus. They become the line cutters and cookie snatchers in our lives and can make us feel small, unseen, or not cared about. Sometimes in life, we *ourselves* have been the cutters and snatchers when a fear of not being accounted for or valued enough has resulted in us acting selfishly, greedily, or harshly. However, when you have an intrinsic belief in your worth, it is a lot harder for the things of this world to have a lasting impact on you, and it makes it a lot easier to let go of the moments where you are slighted.

Why would I get stuck on whether or not someone likes me, understands me, appreciates me, or will provide for my needs, when God does? However, when you have an inaccurate view of your worth and the worth of others, you run the risk of being as far from God's values as you can be.

In Mark 12, a religious leader asks Jesus what the most important commandment is. Jesus replies to him that the most important command is to love the Lord with everything that you are, but that the second most important commandment is to love your neighbor as yourself, and that there are no greater commandments than those two. Later in Luke chapter 10, another religious leader tries to test Jesus and asks what they must do to inherit eternal life. The answer given again emphasizes the importance of loving God first and your neighbor as yourself second. After Jesus has given His answer, the religious leader asks the real question everyone wants to know, *"Who is my neighbor?"*

Jesus ends up telling the parable of a good Samaritan who stops and helps a Jew he finds beaten and left to die on the side of the road. In the story, Jesus makes it known that there were other people who you might have expected to stop and help the poor soul on the road who instead turned a blind eye and kept walking. It would also have been clear to the Jewish audience that the Samaritan who did stop to help would have been someone who was very unlikely to look favorably on Jews at the time and would have had many cultural, social, and maybe even personal reasons to leave the injured person there on the road to die. The feelings the Jews had towards the Samaritans at that time were pretty mutual.

Instead, the Samaritan not only helped the injured Jew out of the road, but they put them on their own donkey, treated their injuries, helped them to the nearest town, and paid out of their own pocket to make sure the person they found was treated well until they were able to leave on their own. The first implication of this story is that when the Samaritan saw the person injured on the side of the road, they didn't see them as the world expected them to; they saw a person whose life intrinsically held value over any earthly determinations on that man's worth.

Let's take a pause right here for just a second. Did you know that our brains are actually hardwired to remember and dwell on the bad things more than the good things? It makes sense; we want to avoid hurt and danger as much as possible, so of course our brains tend to focus on the situations or feelings we have experienced that we would rather avoid in the future. (If you want to study or find more information on it, look into the negativity bias and loss aversion and how they relate to psychological decision-making and processing.) When you aren't feeling valued or when you are feeling abandoned and discarded, you are going to have to look back at your history with intentionality.

Instead of starting the mental exercise of looking for a lack of God's provision and support in your life by focusing on how you think you have been failed or abandoned in the past, you need to think back and try to remember all the times you were supported, provided for, and loved, in ways that undeniably came from God. This is what Jesus is doing for the crowd here in this parable.

In 2 Chronicles 28, a group of Israelites are defeated in battle and sent to Samaria as prisoners. Many of them arrived in Samaria beaten, injured, and naked. At that time there was a prophet in Samaria named Oded who demanded that the captive Israelites be treated better and returned to their homeland. After the soldiers are convinced to give up the prisoners and their plunders, scriptures say, "The men designated by name took the prisoners, and from the plunder they clothed all who were naked. They provided them with clothes and sandals, food and drink, and healing balm. All those who were weak they put on donkeys. So they took them back to their fellow Israelites at Jericho, the City of Palms, and returned to Samaria" (2 Chr. 28:15). Clearly some pretty obvious parallels can be drawn between the historical record the Jews kept and the parable Jesus was telling.

Sometimes we need the reminder that God not only partners with us, but also with those in our community who are also a part of His kingdom. God likely *has* blessed you through those around you in ways you may not even realize because He does it through methods you don't recognize or acknowledge as His work.

In Deuteronomy 6, when the Israelites have made their exodus out of Egypt, there is a call given to remember the Lord and how He offers provision through the service or labor of those around us. "When the Lord your God brings you into the land He swore to your fathers, to Abraham, Isaac and Jacob, to give you—a land with large, flourishing cities you did not build, houses filled with all kinds of good things you did not provide, wells you did not dig, and vineyards and olive groves you did not plant—then when you eat and are satisfied, be careful that you do not forget the Lord, who brought you out of Egypt and out of the land of slavery" (Deut. 6:10–12).

I don't know about any of you, but I know I did not build the house I live in or put in the plumbing lines or electrical wiring to make sure I could have lights and running water every day. I did not grow or kill all of the food I will eat today. I did not build or assemble my car that I use to get around. I did not sew my clothes together or build any of the furniture around me from scratch. Even if there isn't always a physical person in front of you showing you that you are valued, you need to be able to look at all that you have been provided with and realize it is a byproduct of the community that the Lord has given to you.

The other implication that can be drawn from the Good Samaritan story is that, if this is the kind of value we are expected to put on our neighbor, then that is also the kind of value we should assign to ourselves. The commandment doesn't say to love your neighbor less or more than yourself; it says to love your neighbor *as* yourself. If I don't have a belief that I have an intrinsic value, on some level, I will probably have a hard time believing my neighbor does either.

Having an understanding of your inherent worth and the worth of those around you at the core of your identity will be crucial when going into the second part of this study, where we look at intentionally confronting some of the ways we relate to and interact with others. Your actions *are* noticed and *do* matter the same way your words hold weight, and you need to use them with a mind towards valuing God first and people second above anything else that might seem more important, no matter the circumstances or situation.

When you are wanting to evaluate how you view your current self-worth, ask yourself some of the following questions:

1) Have I prayerfully asked God about my worth to Him? (1 Cor. 2:10–12)

From my interpretation of scripture, I believe God knows what it is like to be lonely, abandoned, and hurt. Yet, Jesus died for you. Not even three days after He was beaten and tortured to death, Jesus walked among His fellow Jews, many who had denied Him or cheered for His death, and He treated them as friends and equals. How often do we meditate on the kind of love and sacrifice that truly was and how highly God must value us when confronted with the reality of those actions? Jesus died for the chance for us to be able to have a relationship with God if we wanted it, *because God wanted it that desperately.*

Everything in the Bible that happens from Genesis to Jesus was all done so that Jesus could live and be sacrificed. Every minute and effort since has been a calculated step towards redemption in a way that we will never be able to fully understand because God does care and does love us. It's amazing how, after all of this, we can easily be convinced that God's love is a lie and that we are not worth anything—not to Him, and not to ourselves. When we study scripture and ask God to show us our worth, we can be made aware that even though everything was done for us, *not everything is about us, but that doesn't mean that we are not God's priority.* Life happens, and God is working hard constantly, not just for us but for everyone.

2) Who told me that?

When we look over the list of negative traits or lies that we believe about ourselves, we need to think back and figure out when or why we first started believing those things about ourselves. Maybe the first time you ever believed you were stupid was when you failed a test in elementary school, or maybe you were told you looked ugly in a school picture. Even if it is a vague or distant memory, it really doesn't matter. What matters is that after you started to believe a lie about yourself, every time you felt that same way after, it only reinforced the belief you already had, so you continued to believe it until it became part of your identity.

However, looking back, you are obviously not dumb because you didn't know something in elementary school. Would you tell an elementary schooler they were dumb for not understanding something they just learned? You are clearly not ugly just because you didn't look your best in a photo taken at seven in the morning under a harsh light with a sky-blue backdrop after only being given two seconds to pose before about a hundred more kids did the same thing. Maybe even someone close to you told you or called you some horrible things. Have you ever considered they were lying or lashing out in their own way? What makes you so sure what they said was a defining truth?

Whether it was something we told ourselves, something society told us, or something someone close to us made us feel, go back and investigate: was that true? Who told me that, and under what circumstances? Who benefits from me believing this? Does me believing this give someone else influence and control over me instead of God? If we can look back at one instance of the lie and see where it wasn't true, then we can also look at the reaffirming memories and see how they weren't true either.

3) Do I have some unspoken beef with God that I need to confront?

Listen, hardly anyone wants to admit it when they are mad at God about something because...He's God, but *God can work __way__ more effectively with our honest anger than He can with our passive denial.* If you have had experiences that have made you doubt or want to accuse God of not valuing you, take that memory or those feelings (no matter how messy or ugly) to Him in prayer and ask Him to reveal to you where He was or how He was present in that situation. You may be surprised at His answers.

4) Have I been denying anything to others because I feel like I'm lacking it myself?

In my experience, the things we can be the most harsh or defensive about are the things we feel like we are lacking in or are the things we feel we have been personally denied. When someone asks for my time, and my first feeling or reaction is anger or defensiveness, it's usually because I feel I have been denied time for myself. If someone is asking for understanding, and I feel resentful about it, it may be because I have felt that others didn't extend understanding to me when I needed it or that the person asking for understanding hasn't done enough in my eyes to deserve it (as if I am the best judge on what people do or don't deserve).

My reactions and responses to those around me are much more reflective of me and my inner self than of the person sitting across from me. Those flashes of anger or the desire to wall myself off from my neighbor are a good indicator that I'm no longer operating in the mindset of a worthy identity or an abundant kingdom with enough, but from the mindset of my own limitations when it comes to resources and virtues.

5) Am I feeling undervalued by God because I'm not receiving the things I want in life, especially when I compare my life to the lives of others who seem more prosperous?

Jealousy isn't a good look on anyone, even if it is an understandable emotion. However, we need to understand, God is not looking to buy our love or affections through appeasements. He doesn't want us to love the stuff He gives us; He wants us to love <u>Him</u>. The kind of love that has a price tag on it is a cheap and temporary love that is only valued until something nicer or shinier catches our eye (and everything is cheap and temporary when compared to Jesus). God paid to remove our sin to eliminate any of the barriers that sin put between us. He wasn't buying our affection; He was paying off our debt.

I know it seems unfair when people we don't think deserve it get to live a charmed life. However, the Bible does talk about this at length (Psalm 10, Jer. 12, Prov. 24). We are not supposed to envy the wicked or follow their example. Life is not fair, and rain falls on the just and unjust alike. However, whenever we get into a mindset of thinking about the better things we think we deserve from God, it might be a good time to remember that God has chosen to save us from a lot of what we deserve and be grateful instead. God will eventually set all things right in His time; we just need to remember His promises for us in the meantime and be willing to wait.

Discussion Questions:

1) What or who's opinion do you currently base your self-worth on?

_____

_____

_____

_____

_____

_____

2) How does your relationship with your own self-worth impact your relationships with those around you?

_____

_____

_____

_____

3) What are some of the ways you currently identify lies about your self-worth?

_____

_____

_____

_____

4) How do you feel about others confronting you and holding you accountable to your true value?

_____

_____

_____

_____

5) Do you feel comfortable taking your doubts or hurts to God first? If not, who or where do you take them instead?

_____

_____

_____

_____

6) What are your current three biggest obstacles to seeing or believing in your worth, and how are you working to overcome them?

_____

_____

_____

_____

7) What have you felt defensive of lately?

_____

_____

_____

_____

8) How are you being provided for in ways you might not be noticing?

_____

_____

_____

_____

9) Are you allowing yourself to be convinced that you are lacking something that you already are or have through God? What comes to mind when you ask yourself this question?

_____

_____

_____

_____

Chapter 6
Forgiveness

"We gasp about things significantly less when we remember the grace we ourselves have needed. And still need."

—E.J. Gaines

Forgiveness is a central crux for much of the Christian faith. It is the basis for our salvation that our sins would be forgiven by a merciful God. It is one of the greatest gifts we receive in Christ, an instrument to free us from our sin, and a sign of the enduring love of Jesus. For most churches and Christians, forgiveness is a source of joy and hope to be received when we walk in faith and relationship with God.

For me, forgiveness is probably one of my hardest and least favorite topics to talk about or think about in my faith when I realize *I am going to be asked to give it back in equal measure.* However, if I am committed to following and modeling the behaviors of Christ, I need to be stable and mature enough to forgive people in my life who have done me wrong, even if they never apologize or try to make amends. To have the right outlook on forgiveness for others, we need to first look at and examine how much we have been forgiven ourselves.

All of us have messed up and done or said things we aren't proud of. We have all carried around guilt and shame—that was probably well deserved—over thoughts, words, or actions that we wish we could take back. All of us have done things that we wanted forgiveness for. Not just forgiveness, either, in times where we have hurt people or done shameful things, we want others to understand and have compassion for us. We want people to see how, at the time, our actions felt justified, even if the end result was wrong or our methods to get the things we wanted or needed were hurtful. We also don't want the mistakes of our past or the effects of a bad choice to dictate how people view and treat us in the future. God offers that kind of freedom to us through His forgiveness.

Psalm 103 says, "He does not deal with us according to our sins, nor repay us according to our iniquities. For as high as the heavens are above the earth, so great is His steadfast love toward those who fear Him; as far as the east is from the west, so far does He remove our transgressions from us. As a father shows compassion to his children, so the Lord shows compassion to those who fear Him. For He knows our frame; He remembers that we are dust." God bought the debt we owed and paid for it. I will say it again in case you didn't hear me: *when you accept the gift of salvation through a relationship with Jesus, your sins have been dealt with, paid for, removed, and they are no longer a factor or stain on your record with God*. While our sins may have lasting worldly consequences, the sins of the world cannot keep you from having a relationship with God and cannot stop Him from loving you, blessing you, and redeeming you. The sins and mistakes of your past don't have to hold you back or tie you down anymore, and no one can put that guilt or shame back on you once it has been removed by God.

The dual side of receiving forgiveness like that, though, is giving it. In full honesty, most of the time, I don't want to forgive people, and I resent being asked to do it. There are times when I've been ignored, humiliated, insulted, rejected, betrayed, abused, and treated unfairly by people in this world or their systems and structures, and it hurts. It's painful in a way that I will remember and be affected by for the rest of my life. So, when the Bible asks me to forgive, it feels completely unfair and like I'm agreeing with or allowing those things to happen to me.

The lie I believe about forgiving is that if I forgive, I condone the actions of the person(s) who inflicted the pain and that there will not be justice done for those wrongs. It feels unfair! Why am I held to a standard that they aren't? Why am I held accountable, and they aren't? Where is the justice in forgiveness?

Jesus addresses God's perspective on forgiveness in Matthew chapter 18. The conversation is started by Peter, who asks Jesus how many times he should forgive someone who has sinned against him. Peter suggests seven times as a reasonable number. Back in the day, rabbi's taught that we should forgive someone three times, so Peter's suggestion of seven times would have been considered very generous by the standard practice. However, Jesus responds and says, "I tell you not seven times, but seventy times seven!"

Jesus then launches into a parable of a debtor who goes before his master and is told to settle his account for ten thousand talents. The master who loaned the debt tells the debtor that, if they are not able to pay back the amount, they would order that the debtor, his wife, his children, and everything he possessed be sold to repay what was owed.

A talent was actually a unit of measurement for weight and was considered one of the heaviest units of measurement for the ancient Hebrews. Modern-day experts estimate that one talent equaled approximately a little over seventy-five pounds of whatever the most expensive precious metal was at the time. So, to put it in perspective, conservatively, ten thousand talents would have been worth 750,000 pounds of precious metal. Due to the fluctuating value of metals and inflation, it's hard to say what the exact equivalent from ancient times would be in modern times, but if we were to go to a bank today to ask for ten thousand talents worth of gold for a loan, with the going rate at the time I checked in October of 2022, that would equal out to being an approximate $19,945,500,000 USD debt and rising.[3]

Perhaps another way to explain the value of a talent is to describe its purchasing power in ancient times. There is a record of King Auletes of Egypt paying six thousand talents to Julius Caesar to gain a position as a friend and ally of the Roman empire.[4] In 5 BC it cost Athens two talents to build a brand-new warship.[5] One talent in ancient times was the equivalent of approximately 14.5 years' worth of average wages. Meaning the debtor would have had to have worked for 145,000 years without spending a single penny to pay off the debt, and that doesn't factor in any interest being added to the loan either. This was no regular debt; *it was the debt of nations.*

The debtor falls on his knees before his master and begs for more time to pay back the debt. However, it is clear to both of them that he will never be able to repay what he owes. The master takes pity on the debtor asking for mercy and lets him go, forgiving the debt entirely. After being forgiven his large debt, the debtor went out and found a peer of his who owed him one hundred silver coins (or *denarii*) and demanded to be repaid. The going rate for a single day's wage was one coin, so the peer owed a little over three months wages. When the peer wasn't able to pay back the debtor immediately, they begged the debtor for mercy and asked for more time to pay it back. He refused and had his peer thrown into prison until the debt could be repaid.

Shocked and outraged at the debtor's behavior, his fellow servants went to their master and told him what happened. The master summoned the debtor back and said, "You wicked servant. I canceled all that debt of yours because you begged me to. Shouldn't you have had mercy on your fellow servant just as I had on you?" The angry master then hands the original debtor over to be tortured until the debt can be repaid. Jesus finishes the parable by saying, "This is how my heavenly Father will treat each of you unless you forgive your brother or sister from your heart."

Let's be clear: the peer who owed the one hundred coins was not in the right for not being able to pay back the debt. The original debtor had every legal right to demand the debt be repaid, and the consequences of being unable to repay the debt were also justified by all legal standards, so why is the debtor viewed as wicked and in the wrong?

I am genuinely convinced that there is no worse sinner than a Christian believer. We are the greatest offenders and the biggest hypocrites out of anyone. When I was young and new to my youth group, I once heard a sermon from a guest speaker, whose name I sadly can't remember, and the person speaking was talking about the price of salvation and the cost of sin being Jesus's life. They specifically talked about the illustration of Jesus drinking from the cup of sin in the Garden of Gethsemane before His crucifixion, allowing Him to take on the sins of the world, including mine, before His death. They ended the sermon by saying something that has stuck with me for years:

"Stop filling the cup."

I was floored when I heard it, and I was deeply convicted. It had never occurred to me what a betrayal my continued sin was to Jesus once we were in a relationship. In my mind, all sin was covered en masse, and I had never considered that my continued decisions to sin or to walk in disobedience to God were <u>actively</u> adding to His suffering. It's an even greater hurt when I walk around with the knowledge that I know and accept what the price of that sin is.

Everyone who was born before Jesus was a sinner, but they wouldn't have known what the price of that sin was going to be. Likewise, people after Jesus who never acknowledged Him as the Messiah or who never accepted His teaching wouldn't believe that the price of their sin was His suffering either. But, I grew up learning about Jesus. I was taught the cost. I accepted the blessings that came with salvation, and I had full knowledge and understanding of the terms and conditions of the exchange. I willingly entered into a relationship with Jesus and then continued to sin anyway, and I likely will continue to sin until the day I die.

Some days I really feel and understand Paul when he says, "Out of all the sinners, I am the worst." I think all Christians should understand and believe that. We, more than anyone else, should know the truth, which means that we, more than anyone else, betray it. However, that should also mean that as Christians, we should understand the value of forgiveness more than anyone else and be the quickest to offer it or work towards it compared to anyone else as well.

Yet when we deny forgiveness, we are not only discounting the mercy that was offered to us, but we also reject our job as messengers of the good news to gatekeep that same generosity, freely given to us, from others who have hurt us for whatever reason we can justify to ourselves.

Take a minute and go read some or all of the scriptures below:

Micah 7:18	Ephesians 4:31–32
Colossians 3:13	Mark 11:25
Matthew 6:14–15	John 4:20
1 Thessalonians 5:15	Luke 6:27–31 and 37–38

The sin that exists in this world is the most terrible thing there is. People have done unspeakable, terrible, awful, and horrific things to each other. It is not fair. It is not right. It is not okay. It is not justified. However, when we sign up to be Christians, if we are truly going to follow Jesus and be His representatives who are meant to reflect His actions, character, and teachings, then we need to be prepared to willingly forgive anything and anyone, no matter how bad it is or how much we don't want to.

I'm not saying I like it. I'm not saying we have to reconcile or have any kind of personal relationship with the people who hurt us or who hurt those we care about. I'm not saying that means that people in the wrong should be kept from the consequences of their actions. I'm not saying we even have to tell the person we forgave them. Some of the people we need to forgive might even be dead. But what Scripture says is that we do have to forgive if we want to receive forgiveness and represent Jesus well.

Justice belongs to the Lord, and Jesus paid for the sins of everyone. God *does* think the horrible things done to us deserve punishment; in fact, He believed the appropriate punishment for such hurtful actions was a painful, tortured death and an agony equivalent to that of losing your only child, but Jesus was the one who died. If we claim to be Christians but believe that we cannot forgive or have the right to withhold forgiveness, then *we are perpetuating the idea that Jesus's death was an insufficient sacrifice*. We can't tell people that Jesus's crucifixion atoned for the sins of everyone in the world, with the exception of the person who did us personally wrong. Placing blame on someone else, no matter how deserved, doesn't absolve us of our calling to be merciful, extend grace, or forgive.

As I stated in the earlier chapters, there is a difference between forgiving someone and allowing someone to actively hurt or abuse us or other people. We should **not** have forgiveness weaponized against us to create an environment where abuse can thrive unchecked. The Lord delights in justice (Psalm 37:28) and does not condone the mistreatment of any of His children in any capacity. I openly encourage everyone who can to take advantage of the worldly justice systems we do have to stop continued abuse and hurt from happening, even if you don't trust they will be effective. Use discernment; if you are being abused, please leave, get help, or tell someone trustworthy what is going on.

However, after you are able to find a safe place away from the abuser, you need to find healing and forgiveness so that the hurts of the past don't continue to hold you back or keep you trapped in the mental place of the abuse that will keep you from moving forward in your own life. As we think about forgiveness in our own lives, ask the Lord for guidance and review the following questions:

1) Is my lack of forgiveness holding me back in my relationships with others? Is it affecting my ability to receive forgiveness myself?

When you can't move on and forgive the past, you allow it to impact your other relationships and your view of yourself within the context of those relationships. How often have you projected the hurt you have suffered from one person onto another? This can look like avoiding new relationships because you feel like you got burned in the last one. It can look like withholding love, vulnerability, and trust to an inappropriate level because you are afraid it will be rejected or betrayed. It can look like refusing to submit to new authority figures because you felt mistreated by your old ones.

No one is going to ever know how to perfectly navigate the hurts and traumas of your past, and in that, you get a self-fulfilling prophecy of believing that no one will be able to love or understand you correctly when they were set up to fail from the beginning. You need to ask if you are truly engaging with the person in front of you or attempting to address the person who hurt you by projecting their image onto someone else instead.

In refusing to forgive others for their faults, I believe we also find it harder to forgive ourselves or receive forgiveness from others. On some level, when you hold others to a standard they can't reach, you also hold yourself to a similar standard subconsciously. If I know I wouldn't forgive someone for certain offenses, if I ever commit a similar one, then I will have a hard time believing others will ever forgive and accept me with love either.

2) Am I holding the people in my life to an unrealistic standard?

The world loves to sell us the idea that perfect relationships exist and will never fail. Everywhere we go, we see examples and are told about how everyone in our lives should treat us. Society tells us how our parents should treat us, how a significant other should treat us, how our children should treat us, our bosses, our friends, etc. Our special moments should always be prioritized and celebrated. Our needs in a relationship should always be met. The other person in the relationship should make every effort to consider us first and do the utmost for us. The other people in our lives should always treat us with respect, love, kindness, and understanding. In an ideal world they would. However, we need to consider whether or not this is a realistic standard to hold them to 24/7 or a fantasy of modern media and marketing.

Think about how much marketing is geared towards idealistic families and picturesque romance. Subconsciously, millions of products, platforms, and media are fed to us every day, telling us the perfect relationship is ours, for the right price or with the right amount of effort. When we feel like we have put in the effort and resources towards a good relationship bond, we have a tendency to treat the shortcomings of our loved ones as personal betrayals instead of the reasonable expectation and guarantee of failure that were always coming from a fellow, imperfect human being who also makes mistakes.

Haven't we all had days where we were short-tempered, burned out, and tired and didn't treat the people we cared about with kindness, love, or respect? Yet we expect them to understand and have forgiveness towards us in those moments. Isn't it a staple of true love to know that, *within reason*, we can reveal our worst selves to the people we love without fear of them abandoning us because they choose to love and forgive us anyway when we have our "human" moments? Do you offer the same in return? Are you willing to look past your unmet needs, harsh tones, and rough edges some days to see from their point of view or to open the door for mercy, forgiveness, and better communication moving forward?

No loving relationship should <u>ever</u> be degrading or abusive, and all good relationships should have expectations for mutual respect and healthy boundaries, but no relationship can hold up under the pressure of unrealistic expectations of perfection either. You need to look at every relationship with the full understanding and knowledge that, no matter how much the other person loves you, they will without exception, fail you at some point in ways that will hurt you, and that is normal even if it feels unfair.

3) Have I actually forgiven people in my life, or do I just want to forgive them but haven't been able to yet?

This past year, I spoke to a pastor who talked about how he loved to do marriage counseling with young Christian couples to ask them the question, "Why did they want to get married?" His favorite answer was when the young couple would explain how they felt that the Lord had told them to get married, and would smile at each other, confident they had answered his question correctly. It is not an uncommon answer, if not a little cliché for a young and excited couple. His response as the pastor was always to pull out his Bible and his calendar and ask the couple if they could either go with him to the courthouse right then and there or what day before the end of the week would work best for them to get married.

You can imagine the mood shift! Typically, both people in the relationship would start backpedaling immediately, trying to explain how they weren't ready to get married right then, but in a few months or a year, after having time to figure out more of the logistics, do more counseling, become more established, etc. They would be countered with the question, "But wait, didn't you just say the Lord told you to get married? If the Lord said to do something, why not right now?"

This is a bit of an extreme example, but it makes a good point. In this example, the young couple wanted to get married and experience all of the joy, freedom, and excitement that comes with that, but they aren't actually ready to get married until they say, "I do." They hesitate because there are still conditions that need to be met and preparations made for the big day before they can cross that threshold. It's the same with forgiveness.

I think most Christians can get behind the idea of forgiving someone, but don't know what all goes into actually doing it. We hear about forgiving others all the time, but I think we all know it's a little more complicated than simply saying, "I forgive you." We want to feel free from the burdens that come with not forgiving or maybe we even tell ourselves we have forgiven someone because we know that's the "correct answer" that is expected of us at church.

However, when you think about that person and what they did to you, do you really feel a resolute peace and freedom or are there still deep-rooted feelings that need to be addressed and processed before you are ready to truly forgive them? Do you still use your experiences with that person as a reason to reject others, justify your own negative behaviors, or project your defenses onto other people in your life? We don't actually forgive someone until we brave through the process of unpacking our hurts and surrendering them to the Lord, allowing our outlook and behaviors to change, and moving forward from our hurts emotionally, mentally, spiritually, and sometimes physically.

Healing and forgiveness don't happen overnight, and it is a process that could take longer than you are comfortable with and may need to be addressed multiple times throughout your life. You need to examine if you are actually forgiving people or just saying that you are to make it easier on yourself to move forward with the illusion of healing versus the truth of it.

4) What is my reaction to someone denying me forgiveness?

When someone withholds forgiveness from us, it can feel like a trap that we can't escape from or are powerless in. However, you can't allow the forgiveness of others to be the main motivation behind wanting to repent or to do better. You can't spend your whole life atoning to people who won't receive it, but you do need to take responsibility and be accountable for the hurts you have caused, regardless of whether someone else forgives you or not.

In Christian living, *you are expected to forgive, but you are not entitled to the forgiveness of others.* It is a gift that only they can give when they are ready and not something you can force on them. If you aren't willing to make improvements to yourself because you don't think you will be forgiven by other people, then you need to examine whether or not you were truly repentant; or if you just wanted to be absolved of the guilt and responsibility you felt.

5) What do I not have that justifies me wanting to collect on the debt?

Thinking back to the parable of the debtors, something that always struck me as a little funny about the original debtor was his reaction when his peer could not pay him back. Why does he need or want the one hundred coins? If the original debt of ten thousand talents was wiped without having to pay it back, then this is a pretty wealthy man. I can't even think of a way to spend ten thousand talents worth of money, and this guy gets it all for free. Why was it so important to him to get back the one hundred coins? What was it that he felt he was lacking or couldn't afford that this would make such a difference?

Now think about the debt you feel like is owed to you, what are you lacking that is valuable enough to you to risk rejecting the kind of forgiveness and blessings God has offered to you for eternity. *What else plus the death of Jesus will be enough for you to be satisfied with your debtor and feel that your offenses were atoned for?* What are your one hundred coins?

Please, don't misunderstand. I am well aware the things someone else took from you or did to you might be worth much more to you or may be wildly more offensive than defaulting on a small debt. The person who wronged you might have taken away your sense of innocence or purity, a loved one, your hope, your peace, your dreams, or many other things that would make you extremely jaded, extremely hurt, scarred, and unlikely to forgive the debt you feel like you are owed. However, I want to kindly ask how or where Jesus and His actions factor into that offense?

The trade of the cross was that Jesus takes on our identity, and we take on His. Jesus was innocent, so you are innocent. Jesus was pure, so you are pure. Jesus had joy and peace, so you can have joy and peace. Jesus had a loving Father, so you have a loving Father. Jesus is set to inherit the Kingdom of God, so you are set to inherit the Kingdom of God. These are all blessings that cannot be taken from you. God also understands the hurt of losing a loved one because of someone else's actions (our actions), but in doing so provides an opportunity to have all of our losses redeemed.

You might not believe that to be true, but that is my favorite thing about the truth: it's true whether you personally believe it or not. If you are struggling and believe you are lacking in any way then that is a discussion that needs to be had between you and God, but ask yourself, what is it that the person who wronged you can offer that you would ever truly be satisfied with? Because, more than likely, your offender is humanly incapable of redeeming the situation in ways that would restore what you had before the offense. What could they give you that would ever compare to what God is offering to you freely? As you go through the process of healing and forgiving, anytime you are tempted to focus on what you have lost or the people who caused you to lose it, look to the Lord and ask Him to remind you of His love and sacrifice for you and to remind you of all you have and are in His eyes.

Discussion Questions:

1) Do I have realistic expectations of shortcomings in my relationships with other people?

_____

_____

_____

_____

2) What are the ways I need to seek repentance and forgiveness for myself?

_____

_____

_____

_____

_____

3) Who is someone I need to forgive in my life, and what stops me from doing it?

_____

_____

_____

_____

4) Do I truly believe that the death of Jesus was sufficient payment for the suffering I have endured in my life at the hands of others?

_____

_____

_____

_____

5) What blessings or truths do I forget when I remember or think about the incidents or people that God is asking me to forgive?

_____

_____

_____

_____

Chapter 7
Listening

"In the Gospels Jesus asks many more questions than He answers. To be precise, Jesus asks 307 questions. He is asked 183 of which He only answers 3."

                    —Martin B. Copenhaver

W hat makes a good listener, and why is it important to be one? Well, it might be better to answer that question with another one: How often do we express ourselves directly by saying what we need, what our expectations are, or how we are feeling? How often do we open ourselves up to being seen and known on an intimate level by the people around us? Probably not that often, right? It's the same with anyone else, which means you need to be good at listening to people in order to understand them well, not only for the things they are saying but also for the things they are not.

While imprisoned by the Nazi party in Germany from 1943–1945, Dietrich Bonhoeffer wrote and taught about how he believed Christians should live life together. One of the topics he taught on was the ministry of listening and how vital it is to be a good listener as a member of the Christian community. "Just as love to God begins with listening to His Word, so the beginning of love for the brethren is learning to listen to them. It is God's love for us that He not only gives us His Word, but also lends us His ear. So, it is His work that we do for our brother when we learn to listen to him. Christians, especially ministers, so often think they must always contribute something when they are in the company of others, that this is the one service they have to render. They forget that listening can be a greater service than speaking. Many people are looking for an ear that will listen. They do not find it among Christians, because these Christians are talking where they should be listening. But he who can no longer listen to his brother will soon be no longer listening to God either.... There is a kind of listening with a half ear that presumes to know what the other person has to say. It is an impatient, inattentive listening, that despises the brother and is only waiting for a chance to speak and thus get rid of the other person."[6]

Bonhoeffer points to the heart of something many of us have probably heard of or experienced before: the practice people have of listening to respond and not to understand. In general, the world we live in today is <u>very</u> invested in sharing opinions, thoughts, feelings, and judgements as if they were all facts and absolutes. As Christians who can feel like we have the solutions to the world's problems, it is tempting to talk at people instead of to them and tell them, based on short interactions with them, what we believe their problems are and how they can be solved if they turn to God and pray more.

While there might be an element of truth to your assessments and solutions, this isn't an approach that shows care or love in the ways you might be intending or in a way that is set up to be received well. The core of biblical listening is a willingness to be patient, set aside pride, show kindness, and act in an observant and servant-hearted manner toward the people you are engaging with. James 1:19 says, "My dear brothers and sisters, take note of this: Everyone should be quick to listen, slow to speak and slow to become angry." We all want to be heard and listened to, but what does it look like to be a good listener?

The perfect example of a good listener is God Himself. We can see it everywhere in God's interactions with people. Have you ever noticed how many questions God asks in scripture? "Why are you hiding? Why are you crying out to me? What are you doing here? Where have you come from? Where are you going? Is it right for you to be angry? Who told you that you were naked?" If we truly believe God to be all-knowing, then we know that He already knows the literal answers to these questions. In reality, God has no unknowns. If these questions are not true inquiries, why does God ask?

In my study and understanding of scripture, God does not ask questions to gain information; He asks questions as a way to invite us into conversation with Him. A question elicits the need for a response; *God is offering to listen.* Can we take a minute to appreciate the gravity of that?

Stop here and go read Job chapters 38–41. The same God, who is infinitely more complex than we will ever understand and has more power than we will ever know, makes it a priority to be in relationship with us and actually listens and converses with us. He asks us questions and grants us the privilege of sharing our thoughts with Him. Not only does He open the floor for conversation in these moments where He asks questions, but He also oftentimes takes the position of being the person to ask and listen first, which takes humility, patience, and a heart that desires to serve and teach out of love.

Why would God ask or bring something up unless there was a plan to address it? There is always a purpose to God's actions and words. He doesn't speak just to hear Himself talk; conversations with God that begin with questions lead to actions or deeper understanding just like we saw in Elijah's story when we talked about self-care. In John 5:17, Jesus is recorded saying, "My Father is always working, and so am I." God engages with you in partnership when He listens. He helps drive conversations further and deeper by asking questions and helps you to grow by letting you learn wisdom and understanding for yourself sometimes, instead of just spoon-feeding answers to you.

The start of true transformation usually begins with personal self-discovery. Allowing you the space to have your own revelations and come to your own conclusions about God is a critical step in building your own personal relationship with Him. God is a great teacher who is willing to put in the work to be patient and involved in your critical thinking processes, but that process usually starts with listening.

Jesus perfectly embodied God's value of listening. Jesus was frequently asking questions and inviting people to speak to Him so that He could listen and teach them through showing them He understood them and the heart of their problems. In John chapter 8, Jesus is out teaching at the temple. As He is speaking, He is interrupted by leaders of the law and Pharisees, spiritual leaders acting within their authority, who bring a woman to Him who had been caught in the act of adultery and sexual sin. They demand Jesus tell them what should be done with the woman and reference the biblical law of Moses that instructs that they stone her to death. At first, Jesus ignores their questions, but when they keep demanding an answer from Him, He responds, "All right, but let the one who has never sinned throw the first stone!" The Bible says the accusers, starting with the oldest, walked away.

Jesus did not answer their question the way they wanted; He was not drawn into a debate about the law, and He did not condemn a woman to die for her sins. It is made clear that the men accusing the woman weren't focused on her or her sins as much as they were about finding fault in Jesus: "They were trying to trap Him into saying something they could use against Him..." (John 8:6). Jesus saw the heart of the issue because He was listening to what their real questions and intentions were. They wanted to know what His reaction would be; they wanted to know if He would trap Himself or if He would act in accordance with their application of scriptural law; they wanted to know if He would submit to their authority and teachings.

When He answers, Jesus instead redirects their intentions and anger to the true heart of His mission: to save the undeserving lost by showing them God's love and mercy. When their attention is refocused on themselves and the empathy and forgiveness they themselves need, no one has the heart to beat down someone else like them who is already vulnerable and broken. They walk away from the encounter having learned a lesson and with a deeper conviction and understanding of their own situation and need for salvation.

Jesus then addresses the accused woman, not with punishment or a lecture, but with questions, "'Where are your accusers? Didn't even one of them condemn you?' 'No, Lord,' she said. And Jesus said, 'Neither do I. Go and sin no more.'" He does not accuse her, condemn her, or act disgusted by her even though He would have every social and legal right to do so. He invites her into a conversation with Him and reassures her, gives her grace, and sends her on her way. Jesus listened not only to the questions of the religious leaders, but He also listened to the plight of the woman and made sure to rescue her when she needed it.

Another example of Jesus listening is in Mark chapter 9 verses 33–37. Jesus addresses His disciples by asking them a question: "What were you arguing about on the road?" The chapter says the disciples kept quiet and did not respond because they had been arguing about who among them was the greatest. When the disciples don't answer His question, Jesus responds anyway: "Sitting down, Jesus called the Twelve and said,

'Anyone who wants to be first must be the very last, and the servant of all.' He took a little child whom He placed among them. Taking the child in His arms, He said to them, 'Whoever welcomes one of these little children in my name welcomes me; and whoever welcomes me does not welcome me but the one who sent me.'" If the disciples never gave Jesus an answer on what they were arguing about, this shows that Jesus was listening to them when they were arguing, gave them ample time to ask Him while they were on the road, invited them to ask Him directly, and when they didn't, He answered the heart of their question anyway.

In Luke's recounting of the same instance, he documents in chapter 9 verse 47 that Jesus perceived their thoughts and answered them according to the things they weren't saying. Jesus doesn't call everyone together to let them know their weekly stats and rankings. In order for someone to be viewed as great in the Kingdom, they first have to know and understand what is valued in the Kingdom and then apply it to their lives and actions. At the heart of the argument about who is the greatest is the question of who has the most favor, and potentially the most authority.

The Bible shows the disciples frequently argued about their status and would jockey for positions close to Jesus that they thought would bring them prestige and glory or maybe even Jesus's attention and approval. Jesus instead gives them the answer to the question, "What is valued in the Kingdom of God?" He shows them that humility, servanthood, hospitality, kindness, and love will give them the recognition and acknowledgement that they seek in heaven while simultaneously and kindly turning them away from the desire for power and authority that shouldn't become the focus of their ministry or a source of competition and division amongst them.

It is also notable that, for how much God and Jesus model what good listening looks like, Scripture also warns against the dangers and pitfalls of hearing but not listening. In case it needs clarification, hearing and listening are not the same thing. When we are communicating a need to someone and they don't follow through, none of us are under the impression that they did not physically hear us. We know they heard what we said, but they chose not to take action on whatever we communicated. How often have we seen the example of a parent or spouse asking for help with chores repeatedly, but when the chores still aren't done days later, what is the reprimand that is given? "You aren't listening to me!"

It is the same in our relationship with God. Nearly the entire book of Jeremiah in the Old Testament is example after example of God trying to communicate with His people through instructions and prophets but being repeatedly ignored. Jeremiah often points out that he is not the first prophet to warn the people about their coming destruction if they do not turn from their own ways to listen and obey God.

In Jeremiah 36, the Lord has Jeremiah write out all of the warnings and prophecies He had ever given, from the time when Jeremiah first became a prophet until the moment when he began to write the letter. This would have been *years'* worth of instructions from the Lord. Back in Jeremiah chapter 25, the prophet says he has been giving the message and preaching the destruction of Judah for twenty-three years, warning them to turn from their ways or face seventy years' worth of captivity at the hands of their enemies. When the letter is delivered and read to King Jehoiakim, he burns the letter and refuses to listen.

Later in chapter 42, when the people have been defeated and captured, there is a small remnant left behind that comes to Jeremiah and claims that they are willing to now obey the instruction of the Lord. They want clarity on whether or not they should go to Egypt, and they ask Jeremiah to pray and ask God for direction. "Then they said to Jeremiah, 'May the Lord be a true and faithful witness against us if we do not act in accordance with everything the Lord your God sends you to tell us. Whether it is favorable or unfavorable, we will obey the Lord our God, to whom we are sending you, so that it will go well with us, for we will obey the Lord our God'" (Jer. 42:5–6).

So, Jeremiah leaves to pray and comes back with the instruction that the people should not go to Egypt but instead that God had promised to have compassion on them and to rebuild them where they were if they would stay. However, Jeremiah warns that if they traveled to Egypt anyway, they would die by the sword, famine, and plague, and the wrath of God would continue to curse them. After hearing the instruction from the Lord, the leaders of the group refuse to listen and openly accuse Jeremiah of lying. They go to Egypt, and they meet the fate the Lord warned them of.

The Lord is loving, patient, and kind to His people, but He is also just and willing to hand us over to the consequences of our own actions when we consistently refuse to listen to Him. "Yet you have not listened to me, declares the Lord, that you might provoke me to anger with the work of your hands to your own harm" (Jer. 25:7). Many of the things we suffer from in this world are the direct work of our own hands. We cannot turn around and then blame God for the fallout of our own actions and expect Him to continue to allow us to do whatever we want in disobedience to Him.

The reality of not listening to God is that, eventually, He will stop listening or responding to us when the consequences do come. In Jeremiah 11, God makes it clear that whenever the people do eventually realize their mistake and cry out to Him, God will not listen or relent in His wrath. This is not the first time God threatens to withdraw and refuse to listen to prayers; the books of the prophets are full of warnings like this. In response to the people doing evil deeds but continuing to worship God, Isaiah 1:15 says, "So when you spread out your hands in prayer, I will hide My eyes from you; yes, even though you multiply prayers, I will not listen. Your hands are covered with blood."

These people were claiming they followed and believed in God and were carrying out rituals, ceremonies, or deeds in His name while at the same time acting in ways that were directly against what God actually stood for and agreed with. At the heart of the problem were people who were following their own desires and refusing to listen to God and instead putting His name on whatever brought them pleasure or suited their own ambitions.

In Zechariah 7:11–13, the prophet talks about how the people had hardened their hearts to the word of God and refused to listen to His instructions to care for the weak and oppressed and to have compassion on one another, and as a result, they were destroyed. "'But they refused to pay attention and turned a stubborn shoulder and stopped their ears from hearing. They made their hearts like flint so that they could not hear the law and the words which the Lord of hosts had sent by His Spirit through the former prophets; therefore, great wrath came from the Lord of hosts. And just as He called and they would not listen, so they called and I would not listen,' says the Lord of hosts." So how do we make sure we are doing a good job of listening not only to the Lord but to others as it is modeled in scripture?

Let's ask ourselves the following questions:

1) Is my desire to be understood limiting my comprehension and overpowering my curiosity?

All of us want to be understood when we communicate, but sometimes it can get in the way of hearing the concerns or needs of the person in front of us. It can also communicate to the person we are speaking to that we don't value their input in the conversation and that we don't care about them as much as we care about having things go our way. You can be tempted to talk over someone or begin to be hostile with them if you feel like they aren't seeing your side of things, you think they are wrong, or if you feel like they are accusing you of something in a conversation. However, when you speak over someone or are constantly trying to counter them in the conversation, you are not listening or seeking to understand. *You may be more concerned with being right than righteous.*

There can be a time for clarification, but instead of coming to the conversation with defenses, the need to be right, an answer for everything, or the overbearing need to be listened to first, what about coming to the conversation with an open mind, questions, curiosity, and an intention of wanting to partner with them instead? Keeping this in mind, you need to listen to the answers you are given in their entirety before attempting to provide your own answers and solutions. Learn to be okay with hearing more than speaking. Try to incorporate genuine questions into your conversations with people. Be willing to not be understood.

2) Are my questions invitations that allow me to help and drive discussions deeper?

If you know someone is not in the Christian faith or someone who is struggling in their faith, it can be tempting to offer solutions to their problems like: start praying, start going to church, read a Bible, repent, etc. However, to someone who doesn't believe or who is struggling to believe and understand this advice, it can feel like an added burden of judgment or homework to do, aka., "If you had done more or if you are willing to do more maybe you won't be in this situation."

The same way God starts the process of connecting with us through asking questions, consider this an opportunity for you to do the same when you encounter someone needing the Lord. Ask questions like: How can I help you? How can I support you? Do you want to talk about that? Even if you don't believe in it or ascribe to it, can you give me specific things I can be praying about on your behalf? Through listening you are able to offer the gift of sharing the burdens the person in front of you has instead of giving them a holy chore list in moments of hardship. This can also open the door for them and kickstart some of their own personal self-reflection which can lead to the kind of revelations they need to connect with God personally for themselves instead of through you.

3) Who am I listening to? Do I only listen to those who agree with me?

Once we are in the practice of listening, it's not hard to realize that everyone is speaking, but not every thought or statement is going to be worth listening to. Particularly if those speaking aren't in the practice of being good listeners themselves or aren't in alignment with God. "An unfriendly person pursues selfish ends and against all sound judgment starts quarrels. Fools find no pleasure in understanding but delight in airing their own opinions" (Prov. 18:1–2). We need to be careful of what we are listening to and why.

The world doesn't need any more mindless arguments and squabbles, and there is little use in trying to talk to someone who is intent on not understanding. However, you should be open to hearing a variety of diverse opinions and viewpoints. The Kingdom of God spans continents, ages, races, genders, etc., and _God can use anyone to teach you something new_. You need to find people who will speak the truth, but not just the truth you want to hear. Are you open to listening to opposing thoughts, corrections, or criticisms with an open heart and mind towards receiving what they have to say? You don't want to limit yourself to an echo chamber that just reaffirms the same things and never introduces challenging truths and ideas.

4) Am I taking the time to hear beneath the surface?

Like Bonhoeffer was saying, when we aren't fully listening to someone, it's because we either do not care to show them that attention or because we presume to know what they are going to say, but how often are we reflectively listening to what is being communicated to us versus what is actually being said? Say you have a friend who always has the same complaints every time you talk to them. Their job is a mess, their family is struggling, they are tired, school is stressful, etc. What if instead of tuning out their usual spiel to think about the things we want to talk about next or to move the conversation along, you actually listened and repeated back to them not just what they said but what you heard under the surface? After they give their usual list of complaints, what if you said something like, "What I'm hearing is that you've been feeling over-whelmed and stressed for a while now. Is there something I can do to help? How have you been taking care of yourself in the middle of all of these things?"

By reflecting back to them the underlying topic they are communicating to you, you give them the opportunity to feel heard and listened to. A lot of people process thoughts and emotions out loud better than just in their heads. Giving them the space to talk about it verbally to someone else could be a really helpful factor in helping them break the "spinning the wheels" mental cycle and come to their own conclusions about what would be the best way for them to progress.

5) Am I listening to the person in front of me, or appeasing them?

Especially in a community or leadership setting, there needs to be an awareness of the difference between listening and appeasing. If people are trying to share ideas, input, or opinions with you, but you've already locked in and made your decisions before they began speaking, then you're not actually considering or listening to them. You may just be appeasing them so that you can move on with what you wanted to do anyway.

I think it is perfectly appropriate to set boundaries with people some-times and let them know that you have already made a decision or that you feel capable of making a decision on your own without their advice or input. However, if there is something that is being done that will influence the group, it is not loving or honoring to the other person to nod your way through the conversation just so you can ignore them the second they walk away. It's not enough just to hear them; there needs to be a follow-through with an equal response or action.

6) Do I have stones in my hands because I'm listening to the world and not God?

Anytime the world tries to convince you that there is an "us" and a "them" between people, you need to be extremely careful. People can sometimes be quick to pick out a Bible verse and say, "But the Bible says you shouldn't do (blank) or else there will be consequences." And they are right; there are consequences to all sin, but we need to look beyond what is being said in the Bible to sometimes consider why it is being said.

In Romans, Paul talks about how the law of the Bible exists to make us aware of our sins not to make us righteous (Rom. 3:10–31). God uses the law to make us aware of the consequences, similar to a parent telling a child not to touch a hot stove, because if they are unaware, they run a higher risk of being hurt. God tells us the rules and sets the boundaries because He loves us and does not want us to be hurt or face consequences or hardships we are unprepared for.

However, when you weaponize laws to condemn people, it ends up preventing them from seeing or receiving the love of God, which is the exact opposite of its intended purpose. When you uphold the law as higher than the love, care, mercy, compassion, and grace you are supposed to have for a fellow sinner, you may be betraying the calling to be a messenger who brings people to Christ and instead reject them on His behalf. Do not allow tradition and religion to become your idol like the Pharisees did. Jesus speaks about this at length and makes it clear that there is room to both follow the law **AND** show people the kind of love and mercy that will lead them to God and that neither obligation should be neglected by a follower of Christ (Matt. 23:1–39).

All people are made in the image of God. All fall short of the glory of God. All people of every nation, tongue, and tribe will one day confess the Lord is King. If you are pointing fingers, accusing, demeaning, or rejecting people because they are a different kind of sinner from you, know you will be held accountable for every stone you threw, especially if you threw it in the name of Jesus. God doesn't ask; He commands us to love one another, He commands that we love our enemies, He commands us to love our neighbor. *Throwing the law at someone like a stone is not love.* Do not let the world convince you it is.

Discussion Questions:

1) Do I feel regularly listened to, and what makes me feel that way? How can I make sure that I have been a good listener first?

2) Who have been some examples of good listeners in my life?

3) What are my methods of hearing and deciding to either accept or reject opposing ideas or criticisms?

_____

_____

_____

_____

_____

4) What are some ways I can improve upon my current listening techniques?

_____

_____

_____

_____

5) What makes me want to listen to someone versus not listen?

_____

_____

_____

_____

6) What does spending time listening to God look like for me?

7) What voices am I listening to that I shouldn't be?

8) How often do I ask questions, and what are good questions to ask?

9) How do I switch a conversation from being domineering and assertive to being open and curious?

_____

_____

_____

_____

_____

10) What is the longest I have ever been quiet with God for, and what did I learn in that time?

_____

_____

_____

_____

_____

Chapter 8
Serving

"A good intention, with a bad approach, often leads to a poor result."

—Thomas A. Edison

Serving others has been a core value of many world religions since their foundation. Serving is widely recognized as something critical to community-based societies, one of the core love languages, and a vital part of the church. We are encouraged to be altruistic and serve others, but what I have often observed is that, though using the cover of serving others, *we are sometimes just serving ourselves.*

Serving can become a tool we use to exercise our control over the situations or circumstances we decide are undesirable and a contorted mirror we use to measure our own goodness and value. I do believe people have their hearts in the right place when they are trying to serve, and there are plenty of good things done in the world through the generosity of others. However, the way serving is frequently modeled today is not how Jesus modeled serving and is, by consequence, much less effective. I would like to first address how to recognize some of the ways we may be serving ourselves in an attempt to serve others before looking at how serving is presented in scripture.

One of the first ways I think serving has been distorted is by the expectations we have for recognition or control on the back end, superseding the joy we have in being able to serve on the front end. When you serve it is because you are able to pour out of yourself from a place of *abundance.* You are blessed beyond all measure when you are able to serve others because it means that not only do you have enough resources and time to take care of yourself in a healthy way, but you have so much you are now able to share with your community.

Joy in serving comes from the recognition of God's great provision in your life and the empowerment the Lord then entrusts you with to help others by partnering in His plan in a way that continues to infectiously spread His kingdom. However, I have seen it played out multiple times when it comes to serving, giving, fundraising, etc., how often there is a temptation to withhold if there is not an opportunity for a thank you or a recognition of some sort, particularly if it will be a public recognition, or if there is not an option to control where or how our services will be utilized.

I've seen instances where volunteers were asked to come serve for an afternoon, and there were hardly any sign-ups until a free meal or prizes were promised after the fact. I've seen worthy causes barely receive funding until the offer of a placard or naming rights is given to whoever the highest donor is. I have witnessed promises of large donations dangled in front of charitable leadership, but only if every cent will be spent exactly how the donor says they want it to be spent, which doesn't always align with the needs of the charity. I have also seen instances where people have served or given in the past, but they don't or are hesitant to do so in the future because of the feeling that they were deprived of the recognition they felt they deserved or if they were asked to serve in a way that they felt was beneath them. *Sometimes, we don't want to serve unless we know we are going to be able to receive service in return.*

We have created systems that encourage us to serve by offering to reward us in a way that has now become the standard and expectation of many volunteering their money, time, or other resources. However, this is very counter to the type of generosity and service that Jesus expected us to show. In Matthew chapter 6, Jesus says, "Be careful not to practice your righteousness in front of others to be seen by them. If you do, you will have no reward from your Father in heaven. So when you give to the needy, do not announce it with trumpets, as the hypocrites do in the synagogues and on the streets, to be honored by others. Truly, I tell you, they have received their reward in full. But when you give to the needy, do not let your left hand know what your right hand is doing, so that your giving may be in secret. Then your Father, who sees what is done in secret, will reward you."

I don't know why we would limit the definition of giving to monetary donations. We can just as easily give our time, our food, our personal space, our forgiveness, or our compassion and love. I know it is tempting to think that **all** good deeds should be publicly exalted and praised, and it is good to see people acting godly towards one another, inspiring even, but we need to realize that sometimes in shining a light on our good deed, *we usually also shine a light on the depravity of someone else who needed help.*

At some point in time, we all needed to be served by someone else. How would you feel if someone came to serve you in your moment of need, but they made sure to let everyone know how pitiful you were, how hopeless your situation was, or how desperately you needed their help and what saints they were to offer it to you? Most of us would feel humiliated and shamed, not loved or cared for. By focusing our efforts on making sure we receive recognition for the good deeds we do or for the ways we serve, we may not be setting the Christlike example we think we are. We may in actuality be using someone else's misfortune or life circumstances as an opportunity to bolster ourselves or feel like we've won spiritual prizes.

Likewise, it can be pretty assuming to think that we know the best way to allocate resources and manpower to solve a problem just because we are the ones giving it. If service is meant to be done with the Lord and to the glory of the Lord, then shouldn't it be a process that involves partnership with not only Him but the others He has put in place to help build the Kingdom with you? It is a great disrespect and disservice to the Lord to claim credit for His provision and to think of yourself as a savior in His place. Anything we have to give is only because the Lord first gave it to us. We are born with nothing; we leave with nothing. Everything we have on this earth is only ours to steward <u>temporarily</u>, and the Lord expects us to steward it well and in service to His plans, not our own (1 Cor. 10:24, 2 Cor. 9:6–9, Deut. 10:12–19).

Another way the mission of serving could be misrepresented is in how we serve out of a feeling of obligation. I once heard someone say that they never wanted to work for a company that was only offering to pay them the minimum wage because what it communicated to them was, "If it was allowed, I would treat you lesser." They didn't trust that the company hiring them was caring for them beyond doing anything more than fulfilling the most basic obligations required of them by the law.

How often, when we serve, do we take on the same attitude or mentality? How often do we consider what is the least we can do while still saving face or doing just enough to be helpful in a way that will meet the standard? How often do we think any help or service we give should be met with gratitude no matter the quality of care or effort? Or how often are we only willing to step up to the plate after being asked or coerced multiple times?

If we can all agree that there are plenty of areas or people who need help or who need us to serve them, why is it that we wait until help is asked of us before we are willing to give it? Why do we limit our generosity and hospitality to such an extreme? Is the person across from us receiving this help supposed to feel respected, honored, or treasured after we give them the bare minimum and usually after loudly dragging our feet about it? Are they supposed to feel grateful or dignified when we give them the leftover scraps, cheap trinkets, or what we would have thrown in the trash had they not been willing to take it?

In Luke chapter 16, Jesus talks at length about how we are to treat our earthly wealth we are entrusted with. He ends the chapter telling the parable of the rich man and Lazarus. The rich man constantly lives in luxury while Lazurus suffers greatly and wants only the scraps from the rich man's table. When they both die the rich man finds himself in hell while Lazarus is seen in heaven. The rich man is told he received all good things in his life and did not help or repent. The rich man begs for Abraham to send his brothers a warning so that they might be able to turn away from their selfishness and wealth before it is too late. Abraham replies, "If they do not listen to Moses and the Prophets, they will not be convinced even if someone rises from the dead."

If the prophets of the Old Testament repeatedly emphasized over and over again that it should be a priority to care for the alien, orphan, and widow (Zech. 7:10, Deut. 10:18, Psalm 146:9) and how often not doing so caused God to be angered (Deut. 27:19, Mal. 3:5), should we not make it our priority to care for them as well?

If Jesus gives us the example of a God who chases down His people, who relentlessly pursues them with love, who gives nothing but the best, who holds nothing back, including His only son, who leaves the nighty-nine to chase down the one, *how can we think that serving others out of a place of obligation or as a chore is ever going to properly represent Him, His love, and His care for people?* 1 Peter 4 says, "Offer hospitality to one another without grumbling. Each one should use whatever gift he has received to serve others, faithfully administering God's grace in its various forms. If anyone speaks, he should do it as one speaking the very words of God. If anyone serves, he should do it with the strength God provides, so that in all things God may be praised through Jesus Christ."

When we serve, we also need to make sure to serve responsibly. Applying the "band-aid fix" to a problem we ourselves have no intentions of taking true responsibility for in a lasting and impactful way is not as caring as we might think it is. When we serve or give in a way that isn't engaging with the heart of the problem, we may be doing more harm than good in the situation and leaving it worse off than it was before. We always need to be willing and able to help the person in front of us asking for the temporary relief, but we also need to be properly engaged with finding or supporting long term solutions to the circumstances that got them in a position of needing help in the first place.

We are conditioned to think we are helping by donating money blindly or by just fixing the immediate or visible issues, but that doesn't help build infrastructure, provide stability, break the cycles of poverty or depravity, or truly minister to the person in need. Good intentions and charitable giving have become a multibillion-dollar global industry that can sometimes perpetuate bad stereotypes and attribute to keeping people in poor conditions instead of helping them achieve their own independence and stability. If we are willing to invest in the short term but not in the long term, we need to think about why.

Lastly, I would like to address how we serve the servers. There is a quote by P. J. O'Rourke that goes, "Everybody wants to save the Earth; nobody wants to help Mom do the dishes." It seems to me that there is this pervasive idea in our culture that encourages us to serve those who we have decided need it or who we feel are worthy of it, and in that, we don't consider serving those who we feel are obligated to do the serving.

There is a societal expectation we have of the servants or servant-hearted people in our lives that they will always fulfill their role of caring for our needs or that they will be able to fill in the gaps for us while also being capable of doing the same for themselves. Because we have that mental image of them, we tend to treat their service as a standard and an expectation. People who serve tend to be treated more poorly and with more disdain than most others. They are expected to take the fewest breaks, the least amount of pay, have the most flexible schedules, have the fewest benefits, be the most available, be the most patient and understanding, sacrifice the most things, and do it all without complaint.

Do we realize that if we look at the list of jobs that make the least amount of pay or have the least number of benefits, that nearly every job on the list is a service job? Food workers, waitstaff, housekeepers or custodial staff, childcare workers—all of them provide us with a service and help us accomplish a task we otherwise wouldn't want to do ourselves or don't have the capacity to do ourselves. We are able to eat, go to work, have clean homes and workspaces, have children taken care of, and get the time back we would have spent on those tasks if we had done them ourselves because someone else was willing to serve us.

That doesn't even touch on the work that is done by those who don't get paid for it at all, like stay-at-home parents or volunteers, who may not earn an income from their work but contribute in a way that saves the rest of us funds and resources. "The 2019 CPS CEV finds that an estimated 30 percent of Americans, or 77,949,981 people, reported they volunteered for an organization or association…these volunteers served an estimated 5.8 billion hours with an economic value of $147 billion."[7]

Let's not forget church staff or nonprofit workers either. We outsource our call to be spiritual and helpful in our communities to them, but **many** can struggle to provide for their own families.

With that in mind, I want us to reflect on how we see these people being treated, or maybe how we ourselves treat these people, particularly when they themselves ask for help, provision, or need our patience and mercy. We should not be surprised at all to see how many people feel worn down and burned out, sick of serving, and feeling hopeless about helping. However, Jesus says that His yoke is easy and His burden is light; He promises rest to the weary. *Serving isn't meant to be the burden of continuously trying to draw from an empty well, but a blessing that shows the goodness and abundance of the Lord.* So how do we shift our perspectives and start practicing servitude in a way that honors God, others, and ourselves? Let's start with the following questions:

1) Are we spinning our wheels trying to be God instead of His representatives?

You cannot be all things to all people if your interpretation of that Scripture is that you must be physically, emotionally, or spiritually able to carry every burden for everyone. You do not have the resources, knowledge, qualifications, time, abilities, or gifts needed to do everything on your own, and you are inadequate in that way intentionally. God does not have limits, *but you do.*

When you put yourself in the role of a savior, you are limited to your own capabilities, and you can make serving—or that mental image you have of yourself when you serve—your idol. If your mind is straying to thoughts like, "I always have to do everything, everyone always needs me to help them, I do more around here than anyone, without me everything would fall apart, etc.," then you will notice there are a lot of I's and Me's in those sentences in the role where God should be. Maybe it's a role that has been forced on you by your peers or maybe it makes you feel good to be needed and important in the eyes of others so you seek out positions like that intentionally. Regardless, the focus has been placed on you inappropriately.

Jeremiah 2:13 says, "My people have committed two sins: They have forsaken me, the spring of living water, and have dug their own cisterns, broken cisterns that cannot hold water." You and your idols are the broken cisterns; you cannot give what you don't have, and you can't hold water unless it comes from the Lord. He is a vital part of the process, and you can't be so arrogant, controlling, or self-righteous enough to think you can cut Him out. This is what it means to walk in humility. You humbly serve and act with the understanding of your limitations and reliance on God.

That also means you are able to be confident walking in the authority of your capabilities, knowing those came from the Lord, too. When you serve, you need to play to the strengths God gave you and then trust Him and the community around you to fill in the rest. 1 Corinthians 12 says, "There are different kinds of gifts, but the same Spirit distributes them. There are different kinds of service, but the same Lord. There are different kinds of working, but in all of them and in everyone it is the same God at work. Now to each one the manifestation of the Spirit is given for the common good." God gives you the gifts you do have with intentionality and with the expectation that you will use those gifts for the good of those around you. How do you go about trying to meet that expectation?

2) Whose plan are we following when we serve?

There is no example I can think of in the Bible where God **ever** approaches someone and asks them to come up with a plan for something. God brings Noah the plans to build the ark (Gen. 6:14–21). God approaches Moses and tells him the plans for the exodus (Exd. 3:16–22) and later gives Moses not only the Ten Commandments, but also the exact measurements and specifications for how to build the tabernacle and set up the priesthood (Exd. 25–30). God approaches Joshua and gives him the plans for inheriting the promised land (Josh. 1:2–9). Many times, God approaches prophets and tells them to share His plan of either salvation or destruction if the people did not turn away from their sinful actions. In Luke 1 both Zechariah and Mary are approached by an angel of the Lord to each be told they would be given a son who would play a large role in reconciling the people to God.

God never asked anyone what their plans were or made them figure out a way to accomplish these goals on their own. Why do you assume when you receive direction from the Lord that you have to be the one to come up with the plan for how it will be accomplished? How does the Lord receive the credit and glory when it was your plan, enacted through your resources and through your power?

If God is the one with the plans, then **_He_** is the one you should be following. This is what it means to "give God the glory." It means understanding it is His plans and His resources, not yours. When you give or serve is it after prayerful consideration and affirmations that show the ways you are joining in to help are in alignment with the Lord and His plans, or are you jumping in to do what you think is best and hoping that, because the cause is noble and worthy in your eyes, the Lord will support and bless your plans and efforts?

3) How do we serve the person in front of us?

If God leaves behind the ninety-nine to track down the one, then who is your one? And I don't mean a literal one person, *but who are the ones who are not a part of the "flock"* who need your help and love? Who are the people you need to be willing to allow into your circle of influence, so that you can pour into, serve, or invest in them directly? Do you seek out people to serve or do you wait until the ones with the needs find you?

Until His crucifixion, Jesus modeled a method of service that was to the individual and not just the crowd. How often did He track down the one who needed serving or was approached by an individual who needed help and tended to them directly? Jesus was willing to teach and serve the larger crowds, but frequently He did take an individualistic approach to ministry. He knew people's names, faces, and stories and oftentimes did not seem even remotely interested in catering to what crowds or other authorities expected of Him if it was at the expense of the person in front of Him. In fact, sometimes, to serve the person in front of Him, Jesus was defiant of cultural norms or standards because He knew *the person was more important.* When you serve, are you serving an ideal, yourself, a crowd, or are you looking at the person directly in front of you and giving them a place to be seen, helped, and loved?

4) Are we putting our personal relationship with God as secondary to serving?

Your relationship with God should always be the priority over **every-thing**, and that includes serving. Jesus models this multiple times in the scriptures. When the children approach Him and interrupt the environment, the disciples try to send them away, but Jesus rebukes them for not letting the children be in His presence (Mark 10:13–16). In Matthew 26, before the disciples are aware of His impending death, a woman arrives and anoints Jesus with a very expensive perfume. The disciples are upset and mention that the perfume could have been sold for a lot of money that could have gone to the poor. However, understanding that He is being anointed for His death, Jesus tells the disciples not to bother the woman because she has done a beautiful thing to honor and serve Him first.

At the end of Luke 10, Jesus visits the home of Martha. Her sister Mary came to listen to Jesus during the visit and was sitting at His feet while Martha prepared for their stay. Scripture says, "But Martha was distracted by all the preparations that had to be made. She came to Him [Jesus] and asked, 'Lord, don't you care that my sister has left me to do the work by myself? Tell her to help me!' 'Martha, Martha,' the Lord answered, 'you are worried and upset about many things, but only one thing is needed. Mary has chosen what is better, and it will not be taken from her.'"

<u>Nothing matters to God more than your relationship</u>. Not even serving. Yes, there is Scripture that talks about what you do for the least of these, you do for God, but *if you can't serve the least of these well that also means you aren't serving God well.* There is an expectation to serve, but not if it becomes your idol or lessens your desire to be in relationship with God. That is why Sabbath is so important; it has been built in for a reason.

5) Do we show the love and humility of Christ when we serve?

Jesus frequently shows how He did not consider His position as Christ or His authority and power as something to flex over people or rely on for prestige. Mark 10 says, "For even the Son of Man did not come to be served, but to serve, and to give His life as a ransom for many." Jesus touched the untouchables, loved the unlovable, gave the outcast a place in the story, and kneeled in front of His disciples and washed their feet. He subjected Himself to humiliation, unkindness, persecution, and pain in order to serve. Do you? And if you do, what is your motivation? Why did Jesus? Did He do it out of obligation? Did He do it out of a sense of duty or responsibility? Did He do it so that He could lord guilt over our heads so that He could control us?

The why *matters*. Jesus served and sacrificed out of love. "This is love: not that we loved God, but that He loved us and sent His Son as an atoning sacrifice for our sins" (1 John 4:10). Your love for others, not their love for you, should be the key and driving force behind your service.

The Bible says when you serve, if it is not done in love, then you have missed the mark. 1 Corinthians 13 says, "If I speak in the tongues of men and of angels, but have not love, I am only a resounding gong or a clanging cymbal. If I have the gift of prophecy and can fathom all the mysteries and all knowledge, and if I have a faith that can move mountains, but have not love, I am nothing. If I give all that I possess to the poor and surrender my body to the flames, but have not love, I gain nothing. Love is patient, love is kind. It does not envy, it does not boast, it is not proud. It is not rude, it is not self-seeking, it is not easily angered, it keeps no record of wrongs. Love does not delight in evil, but rejoices with the truth. It always protects, always trusts, always hopes, always perseveres." When you serve, is that the attitude that is reflected in you? Is that the image of Christ that you are showing to the world when you serve?

Discussion Questions:

1) When have I felt the most served or loved? What did it look like, and why did it make me feel so cared for?

2) What does hurtful giving or serving look like?

_____

_____

_____

_____

3) What limits do I put on myself when it comes to serving? Which ones are healthy, and which ones are self-serving?

_____

_____

_____

_____

4) Who is right in front of me? Who is my "one" that needs to be included with the ninety-nine?

_____

_____

_____

_____

5) What is something I have an abundance of that the Lord has given me to share?

_____

6) What are my strengths and what are my limitations when it comes to serving?

_____

7) How am I filling myself up to be able to pour it out again?

_____

8) What conditions need to be met before I am willing to serve?

9) How do I expect to be treated, and how do I treat others who serve me?

10) What does it look like to follow the Lord's plans instead of my plans?

Chapter 9
Leadership

"As a leader, the first person I need to lead is me.
The first person that I should try to change is me."
–John C. Maxwell

A s we conclude this study, the last topic I want to look at together
is leadership. Maybe you don't think leadership is for you, but as
followers of Christ we automatically become His representatives, a role
that asks all of us to show leadership qualities sometimes, *even if it's only
to yourself.* You need to be able to know how to initiate conversations,
broach sensitive topics with love and kindness, steward yourself and your
gifts well, and at times encourage others to do the same. You are called, if
nothing else, to lead by example.

There is plenty of advice out there on how to be good or effective leaders, and plenty of books to read or speeches to listen to that will teach you
how to effectively command a room or build a following. That's not what
I'm interested in talking about today. What I want to look at is the Lord's
expectations for your leadership and the responsibilities you should be
taking on when you become His follower and make Him not only your
savior but also your Lord.

When the Lord calls on people to be leaders in the Bible, they are
often not who you or I would expect to be chosen. David was a shepherd
boy in a field when he was chosen to be king. Joseph was a slave turned
second in command to pharaoh. Many of the disciples were fishermen.
Paul, who was formerly Saul, was someone who had hunted Christians
down to kill them before he was radically converted. God has chosen
again and again the people who, by human standards, are unqualified to

carry out great works and represent Him. The undereducated, the poor, the criminal, the victim, the child, the woman, the man—He equips all who are willing to carry out good works in His name (Eph. 2:10).

If fear of not being sufficient holds you back from being bold in your faith or being willing to step to the forefront to represent God sometimes, understand this is probably a limitation you have put on yourself.

Leadership does not have to look like taking on an administrative or authoritative role in the lives of others. This definition can actually be very limiting and can create an environment where people try to promote themselves or climb a ladder to the top to ensure power or favor like the disciples often tried to do. Leaders can be authority figures, but they can also be the person who inspires others, a person who is willing to consider the group before themselves, the person who is willing to take the first action step, or sometimes the person willing to speak out against injustice.

I believe that Jesus models and instructs us on the leadership potential we do have, but few of us walk in it because it doesn't look like leadership the way we might define it or maybe because the idea of stepping up or out in those ways feels intimidating. However, we are given free will in the Kingdom of God because we are not only His children but also His partners and co-heirs with Christ (Rom. 8:17). **Every day** you wake up and have the opportunity to completely change your life or the life of someone else. The Lord gives you the power to control your actions, reactions, emotions, and, oftentimes, the direction of your day. *What are you currently doing with that power*, and if you are choosing to live the Christian life, what does it look like to have God integrated with your free will?

I understand that for some the answer is that God is the ultimate, supreme overlord, and we are incapable of doing anything more than waiting for Him to direct our every step and decision. God is over us in all things and is expected to rule with absolute authority. That's fine, and not completely baseless, but what is our role in that kind of relationship? Where is the partnership and free will? Where is our responsibility? Where is our accountability? You can't honestly expect a real relationship with God to be one where you are a mindless, empty shell waiting on a shelf, *or in a pew*, simply waiting on direct and personalized instructions to act.

God is not the only one who is capable of making decisions, working, or taking action. Representing God as the domineering, impersonal, and distant authoritarian figure or puppet master is not an accurate depiction of who God has proven Himself to be. Not to mention that can be a huge crutch and cop-out of your own culpability and responsibility to exist in this world the way God designed you to. I can't expect God to take every step or breathe every breath for me; I was designed by God to be His *partner*, not His pet or programmable toy. We were given minds, hearts, wills, strengths, passions, and so much more *for a reason*.

If you are waiting for an invitation or instructions about what to do before you are willing to take action, look no further than the Bible. Always make sure it is in context, but the Bible is full of instructions from the Lord that should be followed today the same as when the instruction was first given. If you are unsure about where to start, I would recommend starting with the Ten Commandments:

You shall have no other gods before the Lord.
You shall make no idols.
You shall not take the name of the Lord your God in vain.
Keep the Sabbath day holy.
Honor your father and your mother.
You shall not murder.
You shall not commit adultery.
You shall not steal.
You shall not bear false witness against your neighbor.
You shall not covet.

It might seem like a silly exercise but go through the list above and pray. Going through each command, ask God what He meant by this instruction and whether or not you are obeying it like the Lord intended. Following the Lord should be an active choice and not a passive one. Following each of the commands above takes intentional choices and actions on our part. Some more than others, but don't be convinced you are following all of the commands before you have prayed about it. For example, maybe you have never murdered anyone, but Scripture says that hating a brother is the same as murder (1 John 3:15). Is there some way you are not following the commandments of the Lord because the disobedience is passive?

Another great place to start when trying to grow in leadership is Galatians 5:19–23, which covers the fruits of the flesh and the Spirit. When you read over each list, which category do you fall into the most often? Which one do you fall into when life is hard versus when life is easy? As you go about in the world, which example are you giving, and how is your example impacting or influencing those around you?

Understand you are not always the one who ends up eating the fruits of your spirit. If you are regularly producing fruits of the flesh, you need to be able to recognize it and understand the responsibility you have to lead yourself to better actions, choices, or circumstances in the future. If you are producing fruits of the Spirit, it is important that you continue to facilitate that and to not become passive in your self-leadership. Every moment is an opportunity to produce fruit of some kind, and you can't produce good fruit without care, time, and intentionality.

God is not passive in His leadership of us, so we should not be passive in our leadership, either.

God makes us in His image, breathes life into us, and gives us authority. In Genesis, God takes His rightful place as creator and sovereign, but He tells man to be fruitful, multiply, and subdue the earth (Gen. 1:28). 1 Peter 2 says, "But you are a chosen race, a royal priesthood, a holy nation, a people for His own possession, that you may proclaim the excellencies of Him who called you out of darkness into His marvelous light." Jesus is justly given the role of the high priest and is seated at the right hand of God, but we are also called to the priesthood. Matthew 9:37 says, "The harvest is plentiful, but the laborers are few; therefore pray earnestly to the Lord of the harvest to send out laborers into His harvest."

Any job you will ever have will likely be accompanied by some sort of training or learning. You will need to know who your boss is, what their expectations are, and how to work in a way that will be pleasing to them. It is not much different when you step into doing the Lord's work in the community around you. The Lord needs people who are willing to grow into leaders that He can use to help others, and that is going to take effort on our part to make that happen so we can be good partners with Him in that goal.

Luckily, God has given us the perfect example of how to do that in Jesus. We are to follow the teachings of Jesus and lead people in the ways He did. So, how does Jesus expect us to lead? How did He model His leadership style? Let's review some of the following questions below:

1) Do you know how to be a good follower?

There is a quote by Aristotle that says, "He who cannot be a good follower cannot be a good leader." Jesus was the Christ, but He showed Himself to be an excellent follower. Frequently in the scriptures, Jesus prays, shows to have a deep and thorough understanding of the scriptures, takes time to rest, gives glory to God in all things, and defers to the Father's will over His own.

Jesus knew what it meant to humble Himself to the will of the Father and what it looked like to be in relationship with God, not just servitude. To be a good leader, you need to know how to pursue God above your own ambitions and desires. You need to be humble enough to know your own shortcomings and understand you need to work with God to accomplish *His* goals and not yours.

2) Do you know who God is?

You can't follow Him if you don't know Him, and you can't work with Him if you don't understand His will. You learn His will by spending time with Him, by learning His scriptures, and by studying His character until you can act as an extension of His will through an active and living relationship with Him. In this endeavor in particular, I would encourage everyone to get to know God on an intimate and personal level, not just through the teachings and experiences of others. Go to the source directly yourself.

Stop getting it second- or thirdhand.

If you really want to know who God is, you have to set aside your preconceived ideas about who He is and how He operates. God is never going to fully be who we expect Him to be, and He's not going to do things the way we expect Him to either. He is a living God, a great teacher who is patient and loving, a wonderful counselor, and an everlasting father. You need to let Him show you who He is for Himself if you ever want to be able to truly love and trust Him enough to lead you.

My understanding of scripture is that God doesn't want you to follow Him because you are forced to. He wants you to follow Him because you want to, because after experiencing Him for yourself, you see that He is the only one worthy and capable of the position. God isn't afraid that He won't measure up or that He isn't fit for the job. You need to make yourself teachable so that God has the room to mold you into the person you need to be to live freely and help others do the same.

3) Do you treat those around you like equal children of God?

One role we can take on, as leaders appointed by Christ, is to care for those around us, regardless of their lives or circumstances, and make it easier for them to experience the Kingdom of God, not harder. In Matthew 13, Jesus tells the parable of the weeds:

> Jesus told them another parable: The kingdom of heaven is like a man who sowed good seed in his field. But while everyone was sleeping, his enemy came and sowed weeds among the wheat, and went away. When the wheat sprouted and formed heads, then the weeds also appeared. The owner's servants came to him and said, "Sir, didn't you sow good seed in your field? Where then did the weeds come from?" "An enemy did this," he replied. The servants asked him, "Do you want us to go and pull them up?" "No," he answered, "because while you are pulling the weeds, you may uproot the wheat with them. Let both grow together until the harvest. At that time, I will tell the harvesters: 'First collect the weeds and tie them in bundles to be burned; then gather the wheat and bring it into my barn.'"

The disciples later ask Jesus to explain the parable, and He clarifies that He is the sower of the good seed, the enemy is the sower of the bad seed, the harvest time is the end of the age, and the harvesters are the angels.

In my interpretation, that would make us—as followers, leaders, and representatives of Christ—both the servants and the crop. If you will notice, it is not the servant's job to judge the good crop from the bad one; the instruction that is given is for the servants to tend to all the plants equally until the harvest is ready. Every single person Jesus interacted with on this earth was wrong, offensive, ignorant, and sinful. How did He love, value, and treat them? As servants and leaders in the kingdom of heaven, the expectation for us is the same.

There is a quote by Charles Spurgeon that says, "If sinners be damned, at least let them leap to Hell over our dead bodies. And if they perish, let them perish with our arms wrapped about their knees, imploring them to stay. If Hell must be filled, let it be filled in the teeth of our exertions, and let not one go unwarned and unprayed for." The goal of ministry is to give people around us the message that they are loved, valuable, and wanted in the Kingdom of God, not saying "good riddance" and handing them one-way tickets to hell.

We need to give everyone the opportunity to learn that and to experience God for themselves. _It is not our job, nor are we qualified to determine who is allowed in and who is not._ As a leader, you need to ask yourself: are you actively trying to help those around you grow to their full potential by encouraging them to experience the love, care, and healing of God, or have you decided that some of those around you are the weeds? Are you trying to keep them and their perceived afflictions separate from those you've decided are the wheat?

4) Do you intercede on behalf of others?

Another way we are expected to serve in leadership is to pray intercessory prayers for each other and to be a safe place of confession for one another. The way that Jesus advocates for us, we also need to be advocating for each other. Prayer is your most direct line of communication with God, and you need to take advantage of it. James 5 says, "Is anyone among you suffering? Let him pray. Is anyone cheerful? Let him sing praise. Is anyone among you sick? Let him call for the elders of the church, and let them pray over him, anointing him with oil in the name of the Lord. And the prayer of faith will save the one who is sick, and the Lord will raise him up. And if he has committed sins, he will be forgiven. Therefore, confess your sins to one another and pray for one another, that you may be healed. The prayer of a righteous person has great power as it is working." In order to be able to pray for others or be a safe space for confession, you first have to establish yourself as a trusting, listening, loving, and non-condemning person.

I have found that most people want to be good and want to do the right things but struggle to do them out of a place of fear rather than malice. Fear can cause people to hide, lash out, isolate themselves, act defensively, or act harshly. As a leader, you need to be able to see beyond their fear and anger, *and sometimes your own*, to the person the Lord loves. Interceding is not only an action of prayer; sometimes it is a literal action where you intervene on another person's behalf to help or love them in the way Jesus would. There is a poem attributed to St. Teresa of Avila that talks about the importance of acting as the Lord would towards others:

Christ has no body but yours,
No hands, no feet on earth but yours,
Yours are the eyes with which He looks
Compassion on this world,
Yours are the feet with which He walks to do good,
Yours are the hands with which He blesses all the world.
Yours are the hands, yours are the feet,
Yours are the eyes, you are His body.
Christ has no body now but yours,
No hands, no feet on earth but yours,
Yours are the eyes with which He looks compassion on this world.
Christ has no body now on earth but yours.

You have to be able to take the initiative to be patient and find loving and gentle ways through the rough edges to the heart of the person who needs help, mercy, and healing as much as any of us do.

5) Do you walk with the joy of the Lord?

Like Ecclesiastes 3 says, there is a time for everything. That includes time for acknowledging the goodness of the Lord and all that comes with that every day. It is tempting to focus more on the hardship, the work, the shortcomings, or the faults of the world, but the Lord has made you and those around you so much more than that. You should be able to celebrate life with people and genuinely live and laugh together. You should be able to know how to walk in the freedom of the Lord and to shed the burdens the world will often try to put on you.

The Lord promises us peace and joy, but how many of us are taking the time to seek it out, let alone share it with each other? You have the opportunity to help others see and experience all that life is and can offer through Christ. God is immersed in everything you are and do, as near as your next breath and as far as the endless point of space and time. There is equal if not *more* space for joy and amazement in this life than hardship and woes. Sometimes the best thing you can offer yourself and those around you is the space to just breathe and take the time to see the extraordinary in the mundane and all the ways that we, as God's creation, reflect Him out into the world.

6) Are you willing to view people as transformed?

As a Christian, you have the privilege of giving others opportunities to grow and be seen as someone other than the person of their past. Luke chapter 19 tells the story of Zacchaeus and his encounter with Jesus:

Jesus entered Jericho and was passing through. A man was there by the name of Zacchaeus; he was a chief tax collector and was wealthy. He wanted to see who Jesus was, but because he was short, he could not see over the crowd. So, he ran ahead and climbed a sycamore-fig tree to see Him, since Jesus was coming that way. When Jesus reached the spot, He looked up and said to him, "Zacchaeus, come down immediately. I must stay at your house today." So, he came down at once and welcomed Him gladly. All the people saw this and began to mutter, "He has gone to be the guest of a sinner." But Zacchaeus stood up and said to the Lord, "Look, Lord! Here and now I give half of my possessions to the poor, and if I have cheated anybody out of anything, I will pay back four times the amount." Jesus said to him, "Today salvation has come to this house, because this man, too, is a son of Abraham. For the Son of Man came to seek and to save the lost."

The Bible gives no indication that Zacchaeus and Jesus had ever had an encounter with each other before this particular day. Something that always struck me about this story is that Zacchaeus repents and corrects the error of his ways before Jesus ever actually talks with him about anything. It has always seemed to me that Zacchaeus was already convicted by his actions and was just looking for the opportunity to change, and Jesus gives him that opportunity. *Do we give others looking for redemption the same chance?* Do we, as leaders and representatives of Christ, take the time to sit down with the "sinners," share meals with them, and give them a chance to be seen as something or someone other than the transgressions they are actively trying to move on from?

7) Are you interested in being right or righteous?

Another calling God puts on us as leaders in His kingdom is to be a people who pursue justice and to not do wrong against those who are vulnerable. Jeremiah 22 says, "Thus says the Lord: Do justice and righteousness, and deliver from the hand of the oppressor him who has been robbed. And do no wrong or violence to the resident alien, the fatherless, and the widow, nor shed innocent blood in this place." We've touched on this before, but being a leader often means letting go of what you think is right for what you know God says is righteous.

If you ever find yourself in the position of a leader being pressured into being a figure of oppression or judgement, then you need to recognize that you are being given a *choice and temptation* to take the authority that has been entrusted to you as a representative of Christ and abuse it. God repeatedly takes the side of those who have been hurt or outcast in this world; you should do the same. The Lord will hold us accountable for our intentions and our actions. How we treat people *matters* to God, especially if we are going to be doing it in His name. You have the opportunity to set the example as someone who is willing to be a champion for those who anyone else would overlook instead of another voice against them.

8) How often do you hold a mirror up to yourself?

I once heard of a social experiment where a group of kids were put into a trick-or-treating scenario. There was a note left in the candy bowl asking them to only take one piece. One bowl had a mirror behind it; the other did not. The bowl with the mirror had fewer pieces of candy taken out of it. When the kids could see themselves disobeying the rules, they became self-aware of their misdeeds and were less likely to break the rules.[8] I wonder how often we hold the mirror of the image of Christ up to ourselves to see how much we are looking like Him versus looking like the rest of the world around us.

As Jesus's representatives, do we take the time to look and see how much we actually look like Him compared to how often we are hiding behind Him to justify ourselves? *Real leaders take their duties seriously and are open to true accountability.* You should work to not only hold yourself accountable to looking like Christ but you should also surround yourself with others who will as well. "Brothers, if anyone is caught in any transgression, you who are spiritual should restore him in a spirit of gentleness. Keep watch on yourself, lest you too be tempted. Bear one another's burdens, and so fulfill the law of Christ. For if anyone thinks he is something, when he is nothing, he deceives himself. But let each one test his own work, and then his reason to boast will be in himself alone and not in his neighbor. For each will have to bear his own load" (Gal. 6:1–5). If you are unsure about how much you are looking like Christ, you need to be able to ask.

Lastly, I want to end this chapter with a few thoughts. To be a leader, you need to have the courage to do hard things. You are not called to be a passive bystander in this life. Hard things can include setting healthy boundaries. It can look like being willing to put yourself in vulnerable places or uncomfortable situations to do the unconventional thing when the Lord asks you to. It is setting an example of listening to and forgiving people where others might not have. *All of these can be extremely hard things to do.* There is no demand for you to be perfect, but you do need to be brave enough to say "yes" to God when He asks and to choose to walk and live as the co-heir.

Joshua 1:9 says, "This is my command—be strong and courageous! Do not be afraid or discouraged. For the Lord your God is with you wherever you go." How many times in the Bible can we read the phrase "don't be afraid"? What would life look like for you if you could fully embrace and trust the will of God without fear?

You can do hard things with Christ who gives you strength. God calls us to do the hard work with Him, but He promises that we will share in the reward and that He doesn't abandon us to do it alone (Rev. 3:19–22, Zeph. 3:9–20, 1 John 1:1–10, Eph. 1:3–14). The Lord has been misrepresented in this world, and everywhere I look, I can find people trying to find the truth about Him and oftentimes seeking Him out *without even fully being aware that's what they are doing.* We need to be strong enough to put ourselves aside to show people what God is actually like and encourage them to seek Him out for <u>themselves</u>, and that won't happen if we aren't willing to do the hard stuff.

Discussion Questions:

1) What does Godly leadership look like to you?

_____

_____

_____

_____

2) What does it look like to be a leader to yourself?

_____

_____

_____

_____

3) What does it look like for you to be a good follower?

_____

_____

_____

_____

4) How are you partnering with God, and how is it different from living passively with Him?

_____

_____

_____

_____

5) What do you think Scripture is talking about when it asks us to give up our own lives to God?

_____

_____

_____

_____

6) What is the difference between responsibility and authority?

_____

_____

_____

_____

_____

_____

7) How do you view others differently in the light of trying to be a leader for Christ?

_____

_____

_____

_____

_____

_____

Chapter 10
Conclusion

"For if anyone is a hearer of the word and not a doer, he is like a man who looks intently at his natural face in a mirror. For he looks at himself and goes away and at once forgets what he was like."
—James 1:23–24 (NCV)

Go back to the very beginning of the study and look over the notes you made from the first chapter. You should have three lists with you. The first two lists should reflect the character traits you have currently and the character you are determined to have as the person you know you are capable of being or as the person you want to become. The third list is of the struggles and shortcomings you felt held you back from being or becoming the person in list two. If you did not make those lists back in chapter one, go make them now.

Looking over that list, have any of the topics or struggles been covered in this study? Has this study made you aware of other things you want to add to your lists? If there is still a struggle to figure out what the current roadblocks are for List 3, review the following questions:

1) What ideas or parts of my identity am I scared of letting go of or holding onto defensively?

We are going to be changing constantly throughout our entire lives. Five years from now, you might not look anything like you do now. You will likely have different desires, spheres of influence, and maybe even a different personality, but that is *okay*. You don't have to have the same favorite color, sense of style, friends, dreams, or ambitions that you have had in the past or that you have right now. *You don't owe loyalty or allegiance to any part of your identity that isn't rooted in God.*

Don't get me wrong, there are certain aspects of your identity that will probably always remain the same because you like those parts of yourself, just as there will always be certain people in your life because you want them there. Not everything HAS to change, but if there is something about yourself that you want to change because you are outgrowing it gradually over time, you are allowed to change it, especially if it is something holding you back from what God is calling you to be.

2) What is my heart posture, and what drives me to action?

What are the motivating factors that get you up in the morning? Why do you do the things that you do? Are you afraid that if you didn't do them, you would fail or upset someone? Are you trying to prove something to someone? Do you chase after a sense of accomplishment and victory? Are you attempting to avoid some unforeseen or imagined consequences? Are you pursuing being right or righteous?

Always be trying to ask yourself some form of the question: Why am I doing this, and does it align with the Lord? Do I feel confident and secure in my motivations? What does cultivating an unmovable identity rooted in peace, partnership, and security look like for me?

3) What are some consequences I have faced or anticipate facing that I don't like or that I'm not comfortable with when it comes to change?

If you change absolutely nothing about your life, picture where you will be a few years down the line. Is this the life you want to have? Are you the person you want to be? Do you feel confident in yourself and in your relationships? Do you feel like you have a purpose and that it is being fulfilled?

When you are finished, look over each of the lists. List 2 represents the Determined Character from Chapter One. This is the type of person we would like to commit to being in spite of worldly influence or life circumstances. List 3 represents the Intentional Confrontation which are the identified limitations that stunt your growth as a person and possibly hold you back from becoming or having the determined character described in List 2. Now is the time for Step 4 of the self-image cycle: Affirming Growth.

Starting over with healthy reflection, there is no singular method of reflection that anyone has to follow. Some people are able to process their ideas internally; other people like journaling to be able to visualize their thoughts. There's always the option to take some of these questions to a trusted person in your life and talk through them verbally. Be aware that we may return to the healthy reflection step over the same topic multiple times on our growth journey. *There is no need or urgency to think through everything all at once or only one time.* Particularly over some of the harder topics, it may be something you continue to work on throughout your life.

The ultimate goal is not to "fix" you; we are whole people just as we are now. The goal is to give yourself the tools you need to become the person you want to be, but no one should have the expectation that it will happen overnight. It took a lifetime for us to become the people we are now; some things will take time to untangle and reorganize into something we can work with.

Finally, moving forward to the reaffirming action step. Once you have thought through what needs to change, start making changes, and make those changes in a way that aligns with your determined character. If you are going to do something, you need to do it and do it right. Your method doesn't have to be perfect, your results don't have to be instant, *but they do deserve your best effort.*

You are the only one who can determine what your action steps will be, because you are the only one capable of carrying them out. The people we surround ourselves with may be able to encourage us and help us significantly at this stage, but no one can do this for us. When trying to come up with action steps that will affirm the determined character, think through the following questions:

1) What is a hard thing I need to start doing now?

You've got metal. Trust me, it's there. We just need to start testing it and refining it. The easiest way to do that is to intentionally set ourselves up to be challenged. Let's not wait for life to do it for us if we can help it.

Test yourself in healthy ways to see if you have what it takes to conquer the obstacle you are trying to overcome. If you don't, no sweat; go hone yourself a little more, come back, and try again. Most hard things will not be achieved on the first attempt. Try to think of the obstacle a little differently each time you engage it. Can it be approached from a different angle? Will you need community help or resources to overcome it? What do you do when you get stuck or hit a dead end? What is the plan if you fail? What is the plan if you succeed? Is God appropriately and intimately involved in the process?

You can overcome the hard things in your life, and if you don't have a hard thing, start challenging yourself to find one. If you have already overcome a hard thing, take a look at how you overcame it. Are you happy with the process and the results? Do you feel confident going on to tackle the *next* hard thing?

2) What is something I have known I have needed to change, but I haven't pulled the trigger on yet?

Maybe you have known for a while that it is time for you to quit that job, end that relationship, set that boundary, or kick that bad habit. You know it's not what you want, and you know it's not aligned with the Lord. If it is not growing you or refining you, it's not going to get better over time. Why are you holding on to it? What is the fear in letting it go?

If you know what you are supposed to do, just do it. Now that you are an adult, no one is going to come around and give you permission. Outside of God, you are the main authority figure in your life now. Start acting in that authority and make decisions that will change the outcome if you know you have already outgrown your current situation.

3) Am I making prayer a priority in my life?

I don't think I can overemphasize how important prayer is. The Bible says that we are to be constantly in prayer (1 Thess. 5:17), but what does that look like in the day to day?

Prayer can actually look much different than how we might have experienced it growing up. Most people I know pray with a structure that goes something like this: "Dear God…whatever you want to say… Amen." The line of prayer is opened briefly, a correspondence is laid out, and then it's closed up like a letter and mailed off until a response comes or until another letter is sent. This is completely fine and definitely what a lot of us are comfortable with, and it is what is expected when praying aloud over important moments or gatherings. However, prayer can look different for everyone.

Some people I know prayer journal every day because it helps them to be able to go back and read their past prayers or to get their thoughts organized on paper. Some people carve out times in their schedule to pray for a certain amount of time every day. Some people find ways or hobbies to engage their physical body, like exercising, hiking, crafting, cooking, etc., in quiet and solitude so that they can focus their mental and spiritual attention on prayer.

Something that has helped my prayer life immensely, when it comes to cultivating my personal relationship with God, has been thinking of God like I would a friend in the room at all times. Maybe we get up and have breakfast together and talk for a bit, but then fall into a comfortable silence as we each go about our own individual tasks for the day. When a thought to share comes to either of us, instead of starting back over with the "hello, good morning, how are you?" formal request for conversation, we just pick the conversation back up wherever we left it off. Sometimes I have a question I want to ask; sometimes He wants to talk about something I've mentioned earlier or something I need correction on; maybe something has just been feeling heavy and I just want to talk about it with Him, etc.

God is always with us; *He didn't go anywhere*, and we don't have to talk to Him like He's at a great distance. There doesn't have to be constant talking for the line of communication to be constantly open. God is always listening; the trick is to make sure that we are keeping an open ear out and making ourselves interruptible when it's His turn to talk.

4) Where is my community?

Community is going to be key to **a lot** of things in our lives. Who our community is can literally be the difference or deciding factor for the trajectory of our entire lives.

Sometimes we are not capable of giving our best effort by ourselves, and we will need the help, advice, and resources of those around us. If you have a community you love and trust, how do you maintain those relationships and adapt them to fit with your growth? If you don't have a community, find one, or better yet, *make one* for yourself. Like I said earlier, you are an adult now.

If we briefly imagine your life as a big sports game where God is the coach, that makes you the captain of the team. Now, pick your starting lineup of players. Who has good communication and teamwork with you? Who can fill in the gaps in some of your defenses? Who keeps you humble while also pushing you to be greater? Who brings new ideas to the table and is good under pressure? Who is good at reading the coach's strategies with you to help you pull out the win? Who will help pick you up after a loss but cheer you on at a victory? Set yourself up for success by picking a winning team.

5) Is there someone I can go to for wisdom or advice on this topic?

Separate from our chosen community, we can take the time to approach others who might be older, wiser, or more experienced in this area to ask them for advice or guidance. Not every situation will translate over exactly, but people who are older have experienced heartbreak, challenges, changes, and trials and found a way to overcome them. Instead of starting at ground zero and trying to form solutions on your own, they might be able to offer you helpful advice that would give you a new starting place or a different perspective on how to go about making the changes you want to see. *Nobody knows everything, but everybody knows something.* Most people are willing to share their experiences and opinions if we ask for them.

For the final challenge, now that you've had time to think about what would be helpful, down below write out two action steps you are committed to taking and pray that the Lord would guide you through these commitments:

Action Step 1:

_____

_____

_____

_____

_____

_____

_____

Action Step 2:

_____

_____

_____

_____

_____

_____

_____

_____

Come back in a month, six months, or a year from now and look at these again. Have they been effective? What was learned from taking these action steps? Has this changed anything about your relationship with God or others in your life? What new action steps can be taken next?

As a last note, I want to reveal one last thing about this study. Understand that what we have been doing throughout this study is building a method and foundation for practically knowing how to "go to God," "give it to Him," or do basic scripture study/investigation. For each topic covered in the study, I started by asking the following questions:

1) What topic is the Lord bringing to mind when I pray about what needs to be addressed?

_____

_____

_____

_____

2) What does it look like to engage with this topic in a healthy way versus an unhealthy way?

_____

_____

_____

_____

_____

3) What does the world say about this topic, and what does the Bible say? Are they aligned?

_____

_____

_____

_____

_____

4) How can people be challenged in this area?

_____

_____

_____

_____

5) What resources are available to engage with in regards to this topic?

_____

_____

_____

_____

6) How does the Lord personally engage with people in regards to this topic?

_____

_____

_____

_____

_____

_____

7) Is there something that would hold people back from wanting to engage with this topic?

_____

_____

_____

_____

_____

_____

Conclusion

You are capable of asking these same questions and diving even deeper with the Lord on any questions or discussions you would want to bring to the table. If there is another topic, obstacle, hardship, belief, etc., you want to investigate with the Lord outside of this study, I would **strongly** encourage you to do it.

Asking questions, getting to know the Lord by learning about Him on different levels, studying His word, or even opening yourself up to Him more personally can only help your relationship. The Lord accepts any form of engagement with Him even if it can be hard or messy sometimes. _That's what growing a real relationship looks like_. Hopefully this study has helped you form some of the tools you will need to continue engaging with the Lord and His word on a more personal and grounded level. Please see the following pages for additional tools and resources that may be able to help you as you continue to learn how to steward your faith and relationship with God.

Online Resources

BibleGateway
BibleGateway.com
　　A popular and user-friendly resource offering Bible translations, commentaries, and reading plans. It also provides verse search, audio versions, and tools for deeper study.

YouVersion (Bible App)
YouVersion.com
　　A great mobile app and website that offers free access to multiple Bible translations, devotionals, and reading plans tailored to different needs and levels of experience.

The Bible Project
TheBibleProject.com
　　Known for its visually rich and easy-to-understand videos and articles that break down themes, books, and ideas in the Bible. It's particularly great for beginners.

Blue Letter Bible
BlueLetterBible.org
　　This site offers Bible tools such as Greek and Hebrew translations, commentaries, and cross-references, making it excellent for deeper study while still accessible.

Bible Hub
BibleHub.com

Bible Hub provides a collection of resources, including commentaries, concordances, Bible dictionaries, and various translations. It's an easy-to-navigate site for study.

GotQuestions.org
GotQuestions.org

Got Questions offers clear, biblically sound answers to many common questions about the Bible, theology, and Christian living, making it a helpful resource for new believers.

Book Resources

With by Skye Jethani
This book helps you move beyond seeing God as a tool for success and embrace a real relationship with Him. It challenges how we approach life with God to help us recognize how we subvert the will of God for our own.

Your God is Too Small by J.B. Phillips
Phillips addresses how people's limited and distorted views of God can hinder their relationship with Him. He offers a correction by describing a more expansive, biblical view of God that reflects His greatness and loving nature.

Out of the Salt Shaker by Rebecca Pippert
Pippert encourages Christians to engage in meaningful relationships with nonbelievers and share their faith naturally. The book highlights the importance of authenticity in evangelism, emphasizing the need to be genuinely involved in people's lives.

Life Together by Dietrich Bonhoeffer
Bonhoeffer's classic on Christian community teaches how to live in fellowship with others. It's perfect for learning how to build a supportive faith community.

The Cost of Discipleship by Dietrich Bonhoeffer
This book challenges the comfortable, "cheap grace" mindset and calls us to live out true discipleship. It's a powerful reminder of what following Jesus really costs.

Asking Better Questions of the Bible by Marty Solomon
Solomon teaches how asking the right questions can unlock a deeper understanding of Scripture. He advocates for moving beyond surface-level reading, encouraging readers to think critically and contextually about the Bible's teachings.

Experiencing God by Henry Blackaby
Blackaby explores the idea of knowing God intimately by experiencing Him in the everyday aspects of life. He outlines how to recognize God's work around us and join in His mission, emphasizing the importance of obedience and faith in the journey.

Emotionally Healthy Spirituality by Peter Scazzero
Scazzero combines emotional health with spiritual maturity, arguing that true spiritual growth cannot happen without addressing emotional issues. The book offers practical steps to achieve emotional and spiritual wholeness by integrating biblical teaching and self-awareness.

A Tale of Three Kings by Gene Edwards

Through the stories of King Saul, David, and Absalom, this book explores themes of leadership and authority. It reflects on how power and conflict shape relationships.

Citations

1. Pew Research Center. *U.S. Religious Landscape Study.* 2014. https://www.pewresearch.org/religious-landscape-study/database/compare/attendance-at-religious-services/by/age-distribution/among/educational-distribution/college/. Accessed March 2022.
2. Telushkin, Joseph. *Jewish Literacy: The Most Important Things to Know About the Jewish Religion, Its People, and Its History.* New York: William Morrow, 1991.
3. "One Talent of Gold Today." *vCalc.* https://www.vcalc.com/wiki/vcalc/One-Talent-of-Gold-Today. Accessed October 2022.
4. Livius, "Ptolemy XII Auletes." *Livius.org.* https://www.livius.org/articles/person/ptolemy-xii-auletes/. Accessed August 2024.
5. Robbins, Frank Egleston. "The Cost to Athens of Her Second Empire." *Classical Philology* 13, no. 4 (October 1918): 361–388.
6. Bonhoeffer, Dietrich. *Life Together: The Classic Exploration of Christian Community.* Translated by Daniel W. Bloesch. Harper & Row, 1954.
7. AmeriCorps. "Volunteering and Civic Life in America." *AmeriCorps,* 2021.
8. Beaman, A. L., B. Klentz, E. Diener, and S. Svanum. "Self-awareness and Transgression in Children: Two Field Studies." *Journal of Personality and Social Psychology* 37, no. 10 (1979): 1835–46. https://doi.org/10.1037//0022-3514.37.10.1835.

www.ingramcontent.com/pod-product-compliance
Lightning Source LLC
Chambersburg PA
CBHW032055090426

42744CB00005B/222